Our Journey

Our
Journey

By
Kathie Heimsoth

XULON PRESS

Xulon Press
2301 Lucien Way #415
Maitland, FL 32751
407.339.4217
www.xulonpress.com

Unless otherwise indicated, Scripture quotations taken from the Holy Bible, New International Version (NIV). Copyright © 1973, 1978, 1984, 2011 by Biblica, Inc.™. Used by permission. All rights reserved.

Printed in the United States of America.

ISBN-13: 978-1-54565-325-8

DEDICATION

To my mom and dad. My mom told me many times that I should put my poems in a book. They both kept the poems I wrote, and sometimes even put them in sheet protectors so they wouldn't wear out and so they could show them to lots of people who visited them. As I worked through the process of getting this book published, I thought of their encouragement throughout my life. My mom and dad are both in heaven now, but I feel their presence in my life.

ACKNOWLEDGEMENTS

To Jesus Christ and my faith in Him.

To the Holy Spirit's power.

To God, for allowing me the opportunity to share poems and writings with people over the years and now to publish them in this book.

To my husband, Les, for his patience as I worked through the process of getting this book ready to be published.

To my family for their encouragement.

To my sister, Karen, and my good friend, Janet, for being cheer-leaders in the journey of this book.

To Anne, Sue, and Ramona for all their hands-on work in getting this book ready to publish.

Thank you to everyone who has been part of this journey!

INTRODUCTION

I'm not very good at drawing. In college, my professor in *Introduction to Art* looked at my attempt at drawing a tree and said, "Keep trying!" Sports are not my thing. One grandson watched me attempt to shoot baskets with him and said, "Grandma, you're not very good!" I'm messy at times and forget where I put things. My husband on the other hand, is excellent at organizing his office, the pantry, his clothes, and even the garage.

But I can write. I don't remember exactly when I started writing poems. It was a long time ago. Words would come in my head, and I jotted them down on whatever was close. A napkin at a restaurant, an envelope, a scrap of paper. I didn't tell anyone I was writing them. Would they think I am nuts? Then one day I took a leap of faith and showed someone some of my writings. From then on, I was known as The Writer. I wrote love poems to my husband. I have written about life. The struggles and ups and downs of it. I wrote poems for weddings, pregnancies, baptisms, and first year books for each grandchild. I wrote poems of encouragement for people going through very hard times. Cancer. Death of a loved one. I wrote poems about faith and hope. And I loved finding the right Bible verse that went with a poem. I wrote silly poems. My stack of poems was getting bigger and bigger. Was it organized? Of course not!

I used to laugh and say I was going to publish one of my poems. That meant I printed a poem, cut it to the size of a store-bought picture frame, and put it inside. Once in the frame and covered with glass, those poems looked pretty good. I loved it when the poem and the timing of giving it to someone were perfect.

Off and on through the years, I pondered the idea of putting the poems together in a book. I looked at my mess of papers, and that thought was overwhelming. I looked at a few web sites about publishing a book. I am not a technical person, so much of the jargon was foreign to me. My mom told me several times that I should publish my poems. She is in heaven now, but at the time, I thought that she was just a mom encouraging her daughter. And I am a procrastinator.

It wasn't until Tsunami Week that I started doing something I had never done before. I wrote blogs (Myelogram Day, Nightstand Prayer, The Day Before Surgery, Surgery Day, and Home & Healing.) Writing is therapy to me. Here is what happened during Tsunami Week. On Monday, June 18, 2018, I had a procedure to go deep and wide on my left arm to make sure the melanoma had not spread. On Wednesday, June 20, 2018, my husband had major surgery on his back.

There was a lot of fear and pain leading up to Tsunami Week. This was my second experience with cancer (the first time was uterine), and this time it hit me much harder. My brother-in-law died from melanoma. The father of a friend of our daughter died from it. I knew it was deadly. Don't get me wrong—I know I am going to heaven. I just didn't want to go just yet. And, my husband was in excruciating pain down his legs. His back had compressed in several areas and arthritis was everywhere. After four and a half to five hours of surgery, the doctor came to tell me and our son that the surgery went well. He seemed amazed that Les's spinal cord had not been damaged. I knew it was a miracle and answer to prayers lifted by so many. On Thursday, June 21, 2018, I received The Call. My surgeon's nurse called to say the margins were clear. The melanoma had not spread. It took me a while to stop crying. On Friday, June 22, 2018, Les was released to go home. It was my birthday!

As a result of Tsunami Week and the writings I sent out, I realized that my experience and the words I used could be helpful to others. A neighbor used one of the blogs at her work. Their leadership team was hurting big time. They needed laughter and encouragement and healing. My last blog ended with a poem I wrote in 1992, called "His Hand." The comments started rolling in. Several people told me they had tears in their eyes as they read that poem. My words, my poem, were speaking to them in a very real way. As a result of hearing from so many, I started learning of trials that others were going through. My praise and prayer list for others has really grown as a result of reaching out to others with my writings and asking for prayers for Les and me.

Until lately, I wondered who was my audience if I did publish my poems in a book? It seemed a little egotistical for me to put it together and hand it to people and say, "Here, read this." Now I know who my audience is. It's YOU! The person holding this book right now. Maybe you need a laugh. Maybe you need a word of encouragement. Maybe you need comforting. Maybe you need to know others have gone through hard times. Maybe you need a Bible verse. Maybe you need a specific poem that speaks to you.

And, I know the timing is right to publish this book now. A neighbor and friend kindly agreed to be the technical side for this project. Thank you, Anne! I don't know if I would have taken the leap of faith if I hadn't known in advance that she was going to be my technical expert! Two other neighbors and friends, Ramona and Sue, said they would help me organize the poems and find the right Bible verse for any poems that didn't already have a Bible verse. I am so thankful for the help from these three women. I knew we were rolling. I made it official on June 27, 2018 when I signed on with Xulon Press. Our Journey is going to be published!

I pray you are blessed in some way by this book. Remember, we are on this journey together. That is why the title is *Our Journey*! I give God all the credit and all the glory.

My favorite verses over the years are *Proverbs 3:5-6, "Trust in the Lord with all your heart and lean not on your own understanding; in all your ways submit to him, and he will make your paths straight."* He is with us on Our Journey!

Each Day!

Each day is an adventure.
I wonder what's in store,
Someone new to meet?
God is always opening doors!

Rejoice in the morning,
Rejoice throughout the day,
Thank you, Jesus,
For leading the way!

And when the day is almost over,
Sitting quietly with your mind,
Bless each person from your thoughts,
Making every day more wonderful—the best kind!

I wrote this poem on March 29, 2007. We are on this adventure together! Enjoy your journey!

TSUNAMI WEEK

Our Journey - Myelogram Day, June 14, 2018

It's only 2:20 PM, and this day has had lots of ups and downs! Actually, this story started several months ago. We had no idea what a journey it would be.

When your back starts compressing, and you have excruciating pain, it's time to do something! Today's journey was the myelogram. Les woke up, and he could hardly move. I have never seen him this bad. His appointment was at 8:00 AM, so it really shouldn't have been a rushed morning. It seemed like time got away from me, and I was spinning a little. What to bring? Google said we might be there for hours, so I needed food. Lots of food. Four protein bars. Well, maybe six! A can of cashews. Coffee mugs. Water bottles. A small cooler with yogurt, a Coke and an extra bottle of water. Did I remember spoons for the yogurt? Yes, I packed a small pantry.

Then there is the reading material. This morning's Wall Street Journal, two library books, and a Reader's Digest. Also, both of our cell phones and the chargers. Anything else? Yes, I needed to eat a big breakfast, so I wouldn't get hungry. I fixed two eggs and two pieces of toast. Les was on the no-eat or drink diet, to get ready for his procedure. I was hoping he couldn't smell the yummy cinnamon toast I just made.

Every move was difficult for him this morning. He had been off all pain medications for a week, and I guess he had hit a wall. It was painful to see him in so much pain. All of a sudden, he started walking to the door and said he was getting in the car. Wait! I'm not ready, and I haven't eaten. He said he didn't want to stop moving until he got in the car. Since it has been hot–hot here, I thought I should start the car and leave the air conditioning on for him. At first, he said he would just sit in the hot car, but he then agreed that the AC was a good idea.

When I was closing the car door for him, he noticed the door to the other car was ajar. That's right. I took things out of that car yesterday and forgot to close my door. My mind is a little swirly lately!

Back inside, it was time for some serious business. I needed to eat, and I needed to eat fast. I started cramming eggs and toast in my mouth. It looked like a scene from I Love Lucy. Then I swirled a little more and made it out the door with my food bag, cooler bag, reading material, coffee, water, etc.

Okay where exactly do we go? No problem. Just have Les play the voicemail again. We knew it was in part of the hospital. We just weren't exactly sure where. For some reason, both our phones do crazy things with voicemails, and sometimes we can't even play them. The one about the myelogram had disappeared. I started to sweat. Luckily both of our brains clicked in, and we called the contact number and got directions. "Go to the Cardiac Care entrance. You can't miss it."

I pulled up to the door and asked Les if he wanted me to walk in with him. "No." He said he was fine. He slowly walked in, using a walking stick for support. I parked the car, gathered all my belongings and hurried in. I walked into the waiting room of the Cardiac Care Center. The receptionist asked if she could help me. If she only knew! I asked if this is where the myelograms are conducted. She said "Yes." I didn't see Les, so I asked if they already took him back. She confirmed he was scheduled for the procedure, but he hadn't checked in.

I started to panic. I went down the hall and turned the corner to radiology. Maybe he went there! I had his cell phone, so I couldn't call him. Then a kind lady who was pushing a wheelchair asked if she could help me. I told her my problem, and she directed me how to get a page over the intercom. I was starting to picture it, "Will Les Heimsoth please meet his wife at the Cardiac Center!" Then a young man came by and asked what I was looking for. I told him, "My husband!" He laughed and said he couldn't help me there! I am sure they both thought they had a real nut case on their hands.

I decided to go back to the Cardiac Center and leave my heavy bags before I headed out to look some more. Miracle of miracles. Les was there! Right where we both needed to be, and I didn't have to send out the All Call!

Time to check in. I asked Les for his insurance cards. He said he'd left them in the car. How could that be? I saw him put them in his shorts pocket this morning. After some more discussion back and forth, he handed me the cards. After we had checked in, I said I would put his cards and the rest of the stuff in his money clip in my purse. For some reason, he didn't want me to do that. It must be the pain! I finally convinced him that my purse was a good place for them. Hospital gowns don't have very many pockets!

Then it was the long wait for them to roll him away for the procedure. More questions, and then more waiting. I knew he wasn't in the mood to hear the funny things from this morning. I tried telling him the sweet messages he was already receiving. Then, I got teary-eyed. Roller coaster of emotions! Also, I found out he would only be in recovery one hour. Then I would take him home, and he would lie flat the rest of the day.

He was back in an hour, and it was over. Yeah! Only one problem. His hands and feet were white and tingling. They said they had never seen that reaction. I am somewhat of a furnace at times, so I tried warming up his hands. More blankets. I sent several texts, and then my phone crashed. I tried using Les's phone, but it has a really strange touch. For some reason, I couldn't get a text to go from his phone either. I finally rebooted my phone and sent out the texts. One text was to the kids. I mentioned that I might need help getting Les in the house. Our son offered to come home and help me. That means driving from downtown, out to our house.

It is awesome to know how many people were praying for Les today. Praying for both of us! Thank you, Jesus! And thank you that he started feeling better. His hands and feet returned to a normal color. And he was really hungry and thirsty. They said he needs lots of caffeine the first seventy-two hours so they brought him a couple Cokes. I had my food bag ready, so he could have a snack along with the blueberry muffin they brought him.

We were back home, and my patient was doing well. I have sent lots of updates. It's heartwarming how many people are lifting us up in prayer. The journey continues. We will find out the results of the myelogram and get a firm date for the surgery. We think it will be July sixth unless by some miracle they can move it up. Then recovery and healing!

I will have my procedure on Monday, June 18 at 1:20 PM. They will go deep and wide to make sure they got all of the melanoma on my arm. Like I said, this has been a roller coaster of emotions.

We have wonderful family, friends, and neighbors, so we are very blessed!

Love to all!

Our Journey - The Nightstand Prayer, June 19, 2018 at 4:30 AM

I wrote this prayer about a week before Les's back surgery, but I am just now sending it out. Tension was starting to mount, and we were having a hard time communicating with each other. I did something I had never done before. I sent Les an e-mail asking the questions I was hoping we could talk about.

Are you scared of the surgery? Or are you looking forward to it? Relief from the pain and more movement again. What is your pain like? And what about the melanoma? It's probably nothing, but for some reason this has hit me harder than the other time I had cancer. Maybe it's because we know two people who have died from it. I want to be with Jesus, just not yet. And why haven't we prayed more about what we are both facing?

Again, I did something I have never done before. I wrote a prayer for us. I knew only God could bring us back together. The words to the prayer just flew out of me. Then I e-mailed it to Les. It was around 1:30 AM. He even woke up and asked if I had fixed some warm water. Yes, that is my go-to comfort drink. Warm water with lemon and sometimes a little honey. I said, "No. I was just doing a little writing." The next morning before he was out of bed, Les looked at his phone. "I have an e-mail from you." I waited while he read it. He turned to me and said, "Thank you." That's all. It was a start. Little by little, we have both been sharing more. But I think it was the words in the prayer that touched our hearts.

I printed the prayer and put a copy on each of our nightstands. I have read it daily and sometimes more than once. We now refer to it as *The Nightstand Prayer*. After reading the words a few times, I realized the prayer is for anyone. You may need to tweak the words a little, but this is Our Journey together. And God is one awesome guide.

The Nightstand Prayer, June 2018

Dear Lord, You are amazing. We have seen Your hand in so many ways lately. We thank You for Your presence. Please fill us both with Your Love, Your Spirit, and Your Joy. Take away any bitterness, anger, resentment, and bad thoughts we have. Help us show love and kindness to one another. Lord, help us take each day as a present. A gift from You. We ask for healing for both of us. Thank you for all the people surrounding us with love and prayers and laughter and sometimes tears.

And when we don't know what to say to each other, help us find the words and the actions that will reflect Your Love. Thank you, Lord! Thank you, Jesus! Thank you Spirit! Thank You, Father! Amen!!

Our Journey - The Day Before Les's surgery, June 19, 2018

Writing is therapy for me, so I wanted to get these thoughts down before Les's big day! The biggest thing I notice is how peaceful Les is. It's like a cloud of peace is covering him. He is usually the one who can't sit still, and now it is like we are both in slow motion.

I know my mind is still swirling a little. One day I left a grocery bag in the car overnight. I forgot to finish what I was doing. Oh yes, the bag had bread in it, but also a dozen eggs! Luckily, they didn't cook or explode in the hot car. Then yesterday after my procedure, I put in the wrong garage code. I kept turning two of the numbers around. I didn't want to bother Les, but I had to ring the doorbell, so he could let me in.

Then, when I went downstairs, I saw there was a small box on my chair with what looked like a bunch of old videos. My first thought was, "Oh no. He wants me to organize this." I just wanted to put my arm up and ice it. He said he'd found a bunch of old DVDs and asked if I wanted to go through the box. My answer was, "Not right now." I don't think he heard me, so he started picking up each DVD and reading me the title. After a while, I realized that he was excited. We are going to have lots more slow time together. We might as well watch movies. The other thing that was so sweet. We looked at each other and laughed. Who would think he would be facing back surgery, and I would have the word melanoma in my life? Yes, we are Ma and Pa Kettle. I have always called our TV chairs that. His is a black leather recliner, and mine is a cream leather chaise. Both are facing the TV. Of course!

Then the activity began. Calls, texts, and e-mails started rolling in. While Les and I were in our chairs, we looked out the window and saw our next-door neighbor mowing the lawn. We found out that the neighbors on both sides of us are talking about a mowing schedule since they knew Les doesn't quite have a realistic idea of his recovery time. Yesterday, he said he would probably be mowing in a week. I haven't told Les about the mowing schedule yet. If I did, he would probably be out there mowing right before surgery.

One daughter brought ice cream for Les and chocolate for me. Our granddaughter twirled and danced and entertained us. Another daughter got my prescription. And our son called to confirm he is picking us up at 5:00 AM tomorrow for Les's surgery date, June 20, 2018. It is our children's way of saying, "We love you mom and dad." And Les and I are very thankful!

Now here we are, the day before surgery. I know what we are going to do. Watch movies! And probably snack too much.

Our Journey - Surgery Day, June 20, 2018

It was a beautiful day, an exciting day, and in the end, for me, an exhausting day. I am going to attempt to share just a few of the beautiful things I saw along the way on surgery day. First of all, I hope you know I am not trying to make this seem like what we are going through is bigger than it is. I am beginning to realize that it is the observation and reaction to our events that is striking a chord in so many people. I am not surprised because we are all on a journey. That is why I call it *Our Journey*.

I was awake before my 4:00 AM alarm went off. This time I was much more experienced. I had my things (pantry) neatly packed into my backpack instead of throwing everything in a grocery bag like I did on Myelogram Day. I am learning! Les and I had a calm morning. He read our devotions while I ate. It was a simple devotion from *Jesus Calling*. The author writes as though Jesus is talking directly to the reader. "You can find me in each moment, when you have eyes that see and ears that hear." One of the scriptures Les read was *Psalm 19: 1, "The heavens declare the glory of God; the skies proclaim the work of his hands."* Such a simple verse that really came true later in the day. Another verse he read was *Jeremiah 29:13. "You will seek me and find me when you seek me with all your heart."* Les and I held hands and I prayed, and then we prayed the Nightstand Prayer together. It was a calm morning.

Our son walked in at 5:00 AM with a smile on his face. Throughout the day I called him my Sherpa because he carried everything. I was following doctor's orders not to pick up anything too heavy, so I didn't mess up the incision on my arm. It is so nice to have my own personal Sherpa!

We arrived at the hospital and things moved smoothly. Nurse Pat took us back. I loved one question she had to Les, "Other than all the things we are doing to you (getting the IV firmly in place), are you in pain?" Les's doctor walked in looking so happy and energetic and calm. I could tell he was excited to get Les's surgery going.

Right before the surgical nurse and anesthesiologist came to roll Les into surgery, Rosemary walked in the room. She is one of the lay care ministers at our church. Her smile and calm spirit filled the room. She greeted each of us and then went directly to Les. She anointed his forehead with oil and sweetly recited Psalm 23 from heart. Then she prayed a beautiful prayer as I had my left hand on Les, and my right hand holding our son's hand. She hugged us and left. Les needed a tissue to wipe his eyes.

Pat gave Les a relaxer drug and said our son and I should hug him one more time because Les would be asleep in about ten seconds. Of course, we hugged him. Les, on the other hand, continued to stay awake and mumble things for quite a while. The subjects were so random that my son and I had the church giggles.

Then it was Show Time. We were pretty sure this was going to be a lengthy surgery because each time someone looked at Les's chart, they commented that he had a lot to fix. More than once I heard them use the medical terms, but those terms were not familiar to me.

The waiting time went quickly. At least the first three hours did. My daughter-in-law had created the perfect way for me to elevate my arm and ice it. My son and I had some good chats and laughs. People called me, emailed and texted. While our son was on a conference call, I wandered next door. The hospital gift shop. Yes, that's right. I went shopping. I found a great plaque with a bike on in, "Life is a beautiful ride" for Les. And this cute multi-colored rope type small platter for me. Souvenirs of our experience!

The fourth hour was starting to drag. Did someone slow down the clocks? Then the doctor walked in to talk to us. He looked happy and excited and calm just like we had seen him early that morning. Doesn't he get tired? Anyway, he told us how pleased he was with

Les's surgery. Then he gave us the heads up that recovery could be a little longer than any of us originally expected.

All throughout the day, I tried to take in the moments. It was nice. While Les recovered, my son and I went to Panera. One great topic of conversation was possibilities of places to go to celebrate Les and my fiftieth wedding anniversary. The whole family is going somewhere! On our way out, my son and I spied something wonderful. A cookie called The Kitchen Sink. We must have it! They put calories on everything now, so he and I rationalized that we were sharing this monstrous cookie. We returned to the hospital and sat in the beautiful lobby looking out at the blue sky, landscaping and waterfall. I thought back to the verse Les read early that morning. *Psalm 19: 1. "The heavens declare the glory of God; the skies proclaim the work of his hands."*

Les is in his room! My Sherpa packed up things and we headed upstairs. Les was pretty alert and looked great. Even when we thought he was asleep, he would often comment on something we said. Ice chips at first and then he graduated to vanilla ice cream cups. I'm guessing he will win the record of the patient who ate the most of them by the time he leaves the hospital!

Our daughter walked in, and immediately, Les knew she was there even though his eyes were closed. She was Les's right hand gal. She fed him ice chips, moved the monitors so he could see all the numbers, opened shades, etc. And she was my nurse to change the bandage from my procedure. She seems to love being involved in medical things. Then our other daughter walked in bringing pizza and salad for me and pastries for my breakfast. And, she brought in lots of energy. She had so many funny stories. I laid my head back and smiled as our two daughters shared funny kid stories. Often Les would comment on something even though his eyes were closed at times. And, he had several comments to me making sure I was okay.

I was crashing, and it was time for me to go home. Our youngest daughter was staying with Les for the night. We know he has great medical care. It's just that he is so strong, and such a quick healer, that we were pretty sure he would try to do things before he should.

What am I trying to say through all of this? I'm really not sure. I think the lesson for me was to slow down and take in as much as I could. And get some rest! And to see God's hands and handiwork. We probably could all use more of all of those!

Blessings to all!

Our Journey - Home and Healing, June 24, 2018

Here are two versions for you to read:

The short version:

Les is home and he is healing! Praise God!

The longer, rambling version:

Hi friends and family,

What can I say? Thank you is not enough for all you have done for Les and me and are continuing to do. Your prayers, your calls, texts, cards, etc. And a huge praise to the Big Guy! Thank you, God!!!!

Les came home on Friday, June 22, which was my birthday! We, of course, had some funny moments. When the night nurse came running in Les's room Thursday night and said, "Les are you okay on your ice cream? This is last call!" There was a wonderful moment on Thursday when my surgeon called me to say the melanoma had not spread. I cried like a baby. Thank You, God!

There were some scary moments. Les started running a sizable temperature, and the nurses tried kidding him about wanting to stay another night. Both Les and I were inwardly saying, "No!" His temperature went down, and he was cleared to go home.

Coming home was a swirl of activity, some fun and some not so fun. The fun part was having our daughter and grandchildren pull up to our house the same moment Les and I arrived. The smiles and energy of those two grandchildren were priceless. They gave hand-colored cards to Les and me and hugged Les ever so gently. Our daughter brought lunch, and she brought a cookie cake. They lit candles and sang happy birthday to me. Wonderful and delicious! Thank You, God!

The not so fun part was tracking down Les's two prescriptions. I had the hard copies and went to one pharmacy, but the hospital sent one of the prescriptions to another pharmacy. Not a big deal normally, but I was tired and maybe a little cranky. Thank you, God, for the nice people at the pharmacy who helped me out and our daughter for getting the second prescription.

Back to the fun part. The birthday and Les coming home from the hospital celebration continued. Our other daughter and family walked in at dinner time with smiles, laughter, and food. I went outside and sat on our big swing and watched our son-in-law and the grandchildren play with the bean bag toss game. I soaked it all in. They all surrounded me when I opened my present from all the family. A beautiful photo book entitled "LOVE Memories with Mom and Dad" The picture on the front was one of my mom and dad. Inside was a lifetime of memories with them. I cried the moment I saw it and started turning the pages. Such a precious gift. They also gave me the full DVD set of Band of Brothers. Les and I started watching them, and they are fabulous. Thank you, God!

They left, and shortly after that, our son and family walked in. The boys had been at a Star Wars camp, and they were coming home after the end of the week program. The boys were in full Star Wars costumes complete with foam sabers. They reenacted their program, and it was so entertaining. Our son gave us a bag full of about ten pints of ice cream with flavors like s'mores, root beer, and more. It was a wonderful birthday!

We are so blessed to have family and friends who love us and support us. That is the best gift any of us can have. Thank you, God!

Les is doing great! I am writing this on Sunday, and his surgery was on Wednesday. He walked outside today and the pain in his legs is gone! There is just that little thing called major surgery that needs healing. At the hospital we were told no BLT (not the sandwich). No bending, lifting, or twisting for twelve weeks. And, I have a feeling this super, duper back brace will be Les's companion for those twelve weeks. Les is healing! Thank you, God!

We have learned so much through this journey. Being able to feel the heartfelt prayers of so many. We now have new friends (a shout out to our new friends and prayer warriors from San Diego.) We have learned about details of things others are dealing with and can pray for them. We are human, and we both get tired and edgy at times. God is ever present in our lives and walks by our side, moment by moment.

This is my last big update. Unless, I have a praise to share. Or a prayer request. Or a great verse to share. I hope you will do the same. Keep the communication going!

I will end with a poem I wrote a long time ago and say, "Love and blessings to all!"

God's Hand

He tapped me on the shoulder,
And softly said my name.
Let's walk this way a while,
Your life won't ever be the same.
And so, I put my hand in His,
And let Him lead the way.
The doubts have bombarded me,
But He's there day after day.
I don't know where He's leading me,
But I know I'll hold His hand.
As God Leads me — oh so tenderly,
Wherever I go, He's holding my hand!

Written on March 6, 1992

I've Got This!

How are we going to do this?
Follow what the doctor says?
When I know for certain,
My patient will disobey!

He doesn't like taking orders,
Others telling him what to do,
He must keep busy.
There's work to be done!

More than once I listened,
And heard God clearly say,
"I've got this.
It's going to be okay."

I had to smile and ponder:
Who am I to question God?
When He says, "I've got this."
I know He has a plan!

Written June 28, 2018

I wrote this poem after we were home from the hospital about a week, and I began to worry how Les was going to follow the protocol for recovery after back surgery. I began to worry. I began to devise plans. Then I felt God telling me that He had this! What am I saying? He has everything in our lives!

"Do not be anxious about anything, but in every situation,
by prayer and petition, with thanksgiving, present your
requests to God."
Philippians 4:6

THE REST OF THE JOURNEY

A Baby Is A Miracle

A baby is a miracle,
It's part of God's own plan,
To share this precious gift,
With a woman and a man.

Such a special child,
Blessed this baptism day.
God holds you gently in His arms,
And loves you in every way!

I wrote this on May 4, 2006. Someone asked me to write a baptism poem for their child. I wrote baptism poems for each of our grandchildren. One grandchild (at age six now) told me that he knew I was at his baptism. I asked him how he knew that. He said, "Because you wrote a poem!" Cute!

"Children are a heritage from the Lord,
offspring a reward from him."
Psalm 127:3

A Broken Wrist

A broken wrist—no problem.
There are plenty of things I can do:
Peel an orange, put on jeans, wash my hair, fold a shirt,
Just to name a few.

This is a challenge, I'll admit.
I'm learning to write with the <u>wrong</u> hand,
And later translating what I scribbled.
Then there's walking on ice again,
And wondering if I can stand.

But I've been patient through it all,
"Tie my shoes! Cut my meat NOW!"
"Carry this basket! Do what I say!"
I know how to command them,
I guess I'm indispensable—WOW!

WHAT I've really discovered
Is the gift of love and care,
LIKE NEVER BEFORE.
Who knows—I might get my candy,
And ask them, "Want to share?"

Written February 15, 1989

My husband and I went on a walk, and I slipped on a very small patch of ice. I broke my left wrist, and I am left handed. That was a problem! I still laugh about me trying to write with my right hand, and then later having no clue what I had written!

"Heal me, Lord, and I will be healed;
save me and I will be saved,
for you are the one I praise."
Jeremiah 17:14

A Kaleidoscope of Colors

A kaleidoscope of colors
Goes whirling by my face,
From tiny to oh so tall.
Some are stumbling, others full of grace.
A slice of life that is so much fun,
An afternoon on the ice,
Spinning here and gliding there,
And for one small price
You'll see it all!

Written May 9, 1993

I wrote this while watching the junior high youth group skate at the ice arena.

"And the one who sat there had the appearance of jasper and ruby.
A rainbow that shone like an emerald encircled the throne."
Revelation 4:3

A Miracle and A Gift

You are the answer to many prayers;
A miracle and a gift!

What a special day this is,
To be baptized as a child of God.
To love Him,
To praise Him,
To believe in Him,
To follow Him,
To have joy in Him,
To serve Him,
To be His child forever!

You are surrounded by family,
Who love you very much.
You are the answer to many prayers;
A miracle and a gift!

Jesus loves you!

I wrote this on June 13, 2015 for one of our grandchildren for
baptism day.

*"I have no greater joy than to hear
that my children are walking in the truth."
3 John 1:4*

A Recipe for Happiness

A recipe for happiness was what I was looking for.
A pinch of this—a little of that,
I thought that if I had them all,
My life would not seem flat.

But God showed me without a doubt,
True happiness is in my heart.
A priceless treasure, that gift He gives,
He planned it from the start!

So, if I tend to wander,
And this smile is off my face,
Remind me of the love of Jesus,
And of His proper place!

Written September 23, 1988

*"Take delight in the Lord,
and he will give you the desires of your heart."
Psalm 37:4*

A Woman of God

You're lively, you're a woman on fire,
Filled with faith—His will your desire.
A prayer warrior for sure,
Always believing in a cure!

I am fortunate to be your friend,
A huge thank-you I heartily send.
The way you listen, the way you care,
The way you pray, the way you share!

You're lively, you're a woman on fire!

Written on October 8, 2008

These words could apply to so many women of God!

"She is clothed with strength and dignity;
she can laugh at the days to come."
Proverbs 31:25

Accept Them for Who They Are

This isn't a revelation;
An idea that's brand new,
But when these things happen,
I will know just what to do.

Instead of trying to change the world,
And make them just like me,
Accept them for who they are,
It's amazing – you will see.

One is going to talk a lot,
Another be extremely bold,
Others think they're the best;
That's what we've been told.

Maybe if we expect them
To behave the way they do,
Our hurts and frustrations
Will dwindle down to few.

Written January 8, 2010

Our pastor used the words "Shake it off. It's not about you."

"For by the grace given me I say to every one of you:
Do not think of yourself more highly than you ought,
but rather think of yourself with sober judgment, in accordance
with the faith God has distributed to each of you."
Romans 12:3

Adventure

We've known you for many years.
We rocked babies,
And wiped away tears.
So many activities,
So much fun,
Working and playing,
Living, loving, laughing, learning.
Life was an adventure!

Now approaching the golden years,
Still confident and caring,
Living, loving, laughing, learning.
Life is still an adventure!

Written December 7, 2010

My husband and I have known this couple for years. Now they are in their eighties, and we just enjoyed an evening with them. What sharp minds! What a classy appreciation for life! Life really is an adventure!

"You make known to me the path of life;
you will fill me with joy in your presence,
with eternal pleasures at your right hand."
Psalm 16:11

All Is Well

All is well because You live within us.
All is well because You love us.
All is well because You forgive us.
All is well because You will never leave us.
All is well because we can love You.
All is well because we can love each other.
All is well because we can forgive.
All is well because You are God!

Written January 19, 2013

I listened to a testimony of a doctor who got meningitis and was in a coma. His chances of survival were minimal, and if he survived, they said he would be in a nursing home the rest of his life. While in the coma, he met God, and everything changed. He saw clearly how much God loved him. He felt God's presence in him. From then on, he knew the most important thing was knowing and loving God. He knew he just needed to learn to have faith, believe, and experience God's love today, tomorrow and forever. He woke from the coma and said, "All is well." Amen to that!

"Be strong and courageous. Do not be afraid or terrified because of them, for the Lord your God goes with you; he will never leave you nor forsake you."
Deuteronomy 31:6

Am I An Encourager?

Do I say enough to show I care?
Are my words chosen carefully,
Or do I scatter them everywhere,
And hope that some will help?

It dawned on me to pray about this,
To be an encouraging soul.
Those in need would make a long list,
If I opened my eyes to see.

What if I just took one a day,
And made a call or wrote a note?
Would it make a difference in any way?
If I gave away my time?

To be an encourager is a full-time job,
The opportunities are endless.
It's from ourselves that we will rob,
If we turn away and miss our chance!

Written June 30, 1989

"That is, that you and I may be mutually encouraged
by each other's faith."
Romans 1:12

Amazing Strength

You walked the path
With your head held high,
Helping others along the way.
Amazing strength, amazing love!

While at the same time,
Your own child
Knocked on death's door.
This happened once,
And happened over and over.

How do you keep going?
Taking each day at a time.
I think you would answer,
Only by the grace of God!

You're walking down the path
With your head held high,
Helping others along the way.
Amazing strength from Jesus,
Amazing love for your child!

Written October 1, 2009

This poem was written for friends who were dealing with life threatening issues with their child. The way they dealt with their own pain while helping others at the same time was amazing to me.

"For the grace of God has appeared that offers
salvation to all people."
Titus 2:11

Angel

How do you tell someone,
You are an angel in the flesh?
So full of heart and soul and laughter,
Your face so sweet and fresh.

Day after day and week after week,
You are the same unchanging rock of life.
So often I would talk to you,
And laugh and forget my problems and strife.

The lives you have touched
Are more than you will ever know.
You have made mine richer and I thank you,
You are an angel from head to toe.

I know God is preparing a crown for you,
With jewels added day after day.
May your life be long and full and happy,
For the angel in my life, this is what I pray!

Written August 5, 1994

Many times, there are angels in our life. And hopefully there are times we are angels to others!

"But you are a chosen people, a royal priesthood, a holy nation,
God's special possession, that you may declare the praises of him
who called you out of darkness into his wonderful light."
1 Peter 2:9

Anticipation

The anticipation is building,
Waiting weeks are down to few.
Will the color be pink?
Or will it be blue?

Tiny hands to hold your heart,
A soul already burning bright.
Could be a football star
Or a soccer girl out of sight!

At this Christmas time,
With gifts around the tree,
Your best gift is yet to come
Soon—Your baby you will see!

Written December 21, 2008

"Every good and perfect gift is from above, coming down from the Father of the heavenly lights, who does not change like shifting shadows."
Psalm 127:3

Are You Listening?

How many times have I scurried on?
So many things to do,
The times are set, I must not bend.
Spare moments are truly few.

Then You prod me to listen to You.
To call, to visit, to pray.
You know your people
And who is hurting today.

And so, may I be reminded,
To listen to my Master's voice,
And may You continue to strengthen me,
To serve You as my first choice!

Written September 7, 1988

"He says, 'Be still, and know that I am God;
"I will be exalted among the nations,
I will be exalted in the earth."
Psalm 46:10

At Times

At times your path may be smooth and carefree,
And it's easy for those to see.
Then there are times,
When your path is rough and hard to bear,
Only made smoother because others care.

Written June 28, 2005

"When Job's three friends, Eliphaz the Temanite, Bildad the Shuhite and Zophar the Naamathite, heard about all the troubles that had come upon him, they set out from their homes and met together by agreement to go and sympathize with him and comfort him."
Job 2:11

Attached to a Cord

A friend for so many years,
What a cute beginning.
Both expecting a child,
Those daily calls
Talking, laughing, crying.
All attached to a cord!

Faith is our bond,
Vacation Bible School and answered prayer!
Miles may separate us,
Sisters in Christ we are,
On earth and heaven beyond!

To laugh and solve the world's problems,
We can do it all over the phone.
I thank God for you
Such a precious soul!

Written January 4, 2010

This poem is about a longtime friendship. Our means of conversation when our children were young was talking on the phone that had a long cord on it. We could wash dishes, clean, entertain, and discipline children all within the radius of that cord.

Do you have a friend who lives far away? Isn't it amazing how you stay connected, especially if you have that common thread of being a sister or brother in Christ? By the way, when I talk with this friend, we still can talk for a long time and solve the world's problems!

"The Lord is my strength and my shield;
my heart trusts in him, and he helps me.
My heart leaps for joy, and with my song I praise him."
Psalm 28:7

Baptism

Today we hold you in our arms
And share the love of God.
He created you so perfectly
And knew you before time began.

May you grow to hold His hand
And walk His way.
May you love Him more and more,
From this baptism day
Throughout your life to eternity!

Written May 11, 2013

*"Whoever welcomes one of these little children in my name
welcomes me; and whoever welcomes me does not welcome
me but the one who sent me."*
Mark 9:37

Baptism Day

Such a special little guy,
You carry a treasure.
And I will tell you why;

Your mom and dad and brother
Love you oh, so much.
Grandparents, aunts, uncles, cousins,
Surround you with a prayerful touch.

God made you who you are,
You are part of His wonderful plan,
He will love you forever,
Upon that Rock may you always stand!

God bless your baptism day!

Written February 7, 2010

"Truly he is my rock and my salvation;
he is my fortress, I will not be shaken.
My salvation and my honor depend on God;
he is my mighty rock, my refuge.
Trust in him at all times, you people;
pour out your hearts to him,
for God is our refuge."
Psalm 62:6-8

Be Still in The Quiet

Sometimes things happen,
Out of our control.
What once was so busy,
Isn't busy at all.

Maybe an illness,
Or maybe a fall.
Accidents do happen,
Not expected at all.

You hear God whisper,
"Be still in your soul.
The quiet is lovely
It's gentle and kind."

If this didn't happen,
I would still be running
And miss this quiet,
Beautiful time with God!

Written June 27, 2018

"He says, 'Be still, and know that I am God;
I will be exalted among the nations,
I will be exalted in the earth.'"
Psalm 46:10

Believing in Healing

I remember the first time
You were sitting in front of me at church.
Wearing a turban with your head bowed,
Your boys by your side.

My heart went out to you
And I knew I would
Start to pray fervently,
For you and your boys.

So many surround you
And cover you in prayer.
Believing in healing
For you and your boys!

Written January 17, 2010

I sat in church and noticed a young mom who obviously was battling cancer. I watched her several Sundays, and then I knew I needed to know her name, so I could pray for her by name. I found out she is battling recurring brain cancer. She has two boys, and she wants to live for them. I looked for her each Sunday. She inspired me just by the gracious way she was traveling this journey.

> *"He heals the brokenhearted*
> *and binds up their wounds."*
> *Psalm 147:3*

Binkie Free

I had a little binkie,
I sucked it all the time.
I went to bed with several,
All of them were mine!

Then one day I realized
How grown up I was.
I could give up my binkies,
The reason—just because!

My mom and dad helped me
Put all the binkies away.
They are proud of me,
This is what they say, "Way to go!"

You can do it too,
It is easy as can be.
Put your binkie in a (box, bear, balloon,)
It is great! You will see!

Then you will hear the praise
"Good girl or Good boy! Way to go!"
You will be proud of yourself,
This is what I know!

Written September 2, 2010

My daughter-in-law asked me to write a poem about getting rid of a binkie. She wanted me to publish it in a children's book back in 2010. She was ready for our grandson to give up his binkie, but she couldn't find any books on the topic. It was easy to write the words, and I could picture the book, but I just didn't know how to do the technical part of making a book. I think I missed my chance because there are lots of books written today about giving up a binkie. It was fun thinking about the possibility!

"I can do all this through him who gives me strength."
Philippians 4:13

Birth of A Child

There is something so universal about the anticipation of the birth of a child. Are you wanting a child and it hasn't happened yet? Have you been pregnant with a child and wanted that child so badly, and yet that child didn't make it? I have been there, and I feel your pain. All I can say is that God will fill the void somehow. I pray that you will be able to share the anticipation of a child with someone or even experience it yourself!

My story goes back a long way. I was teaching high school, and I loved it. However, after a while my heart really wanted a child. I had students who were pregnant. Some had abortions. Others kept their children, and they seemed to be little toys. Okay, maybe my thinking was a little slanted. I became pregnant, and I told the world. I was so happy. I had even resigned from teaching. Then in the early summer, I lost the baby. I was about four months along, and I was devastated. After that, my body and my soul went into a deep, dark place. Somehow, I managed to teach all my classes. When I got home, the sadness would cover me again. It was causing a barrier between my husband and me. My body had shut down, and there seemed to be little hope for a baby. My doctor put me on a medicine to make me ovulate. I could only be on that medicine for three months. I remember it clearly. I was on my last month. . .what I thought was my last hope. It was February thirteenth. I surrendered completely and somehow gave it all to God. About two weeks later, it was time for the pregnancy test. I had done that many times before, and the result was always negative. Back in the day, we had to bring urine samples to the lab. I worked forty-five miles from our home so my husband took it in for me. I taught all day and then returned to an empty house. I went upstairs and read my Bible, and the tears fell on the pages. They were still tears of surrender. Les came in the door, and I hugged him and said, "It's negative again. Right?" He smiled, hugged me, and said, "You are pregnant!" I can't begin to explain the joy, the awe, the total awareness of this gift from God! We went to a local Italian restaurant that night, and I can tell you exactly what

I ate. Throughout my entire pregnancy, I carried that awe of the miracle of a child. That awe has never left me. I had that same awe each time I was allowed to have another child. So now when I hear someone is having a child, I will celebrate with them like no other!

Now I am at a different stage of my life. Each time we received the news of a grandchild, my reaction was the same. I was thrilled to the core!

"Jesus looked at them and said, 'With man this is impossible, but not with God; all things are possible with God.'"
Mark 10:27

Bless You My Friend

How many years have we known each other?
I just know it is a very long time.
Memories of little children,
Standing by our side.

Those days of shopping,
Coffee and lunch,
Now those were days sublime.
We went to France,
Can you believe it!
The Eiffel Tower
And we were there!

Our children grew up,
Had babies of their own.
We love the sound of grandma.
Through it all,
Is a precious strand
The love of Jesus
And prayer for all seasons.

Bless you, my friend.
Bless all you are doing.
Bless the life you've been given!

Written January 7, 2010

Think of friends you have had for a long time. There are so many
memories. Sometimes you don't talk for a long time. Hopefully, the
love of Jesus keep you connected forever!

The original poem had the word kids in it. I changed that word to children because I talked to my ninety-year-old mom, and she said that kids are little goats. We should call them children. That was good enough for me!

Broken Chain

It started with a broken chain,
On a bicycle built for two.
The man and woman standing there
As we were walking by.

We chatted for a while
About their intriguing bike.
A double trike that pulls apart
And seats like comfy chairs.

They told us how they love their bike
And all the fun they had.
We told them we like biking,
With singles and a tandem too.

Then we noticed the broken chain,
Asked if we could help.
The man said he was fine,
He took the bike apart,
Rode the second trike to get the van.

We smiled and said good-bye
To the friendly man and wife.
We walked some more.
Then I realized
God had planned it all!

Maybe someday we'll get a bike like that,
Finding things to do together.
God took the time to show me,
It started with a broken chain!

Written July 17, 2014

Written after a walk a couple days ago. Sometimes I can see clearly how God sets certain things up for us in life. When I realize this, I am blown away by what a personal God He is!

"Do not be anxious about anything, but in every situation, by prayer and petition, with thanksgiving, present your requests to God. And the peace of God, which transcends all understanding, will guard your hearts and your minds in Christ Jesus."
Philippians 4:6-7

Burned Macaroni

When I have something on my mind and it won't go away, I have to do this. Write! Yes, I know it is 5:30 AM, but that is how I roll.

The title of this writing is *Burned Macaroni*, but it is so much more than that. Maybe the whole title should be "Burned Macaroni and Other Things I Learned." Yesterday, after the girls and I returned from a little shopping, I saw something on the driveway just outside our garage door. What could it be? We all took a closer look, and it slowly dawned on me what it was. A completely charred, melted container than used to be microwave macaroni. It's a favorite of several of our grandchildren.

I had a gamut of emotions after that. First laughter (maybe a little hysterical laughter!), then frustration, then complete deflation. Here is the first thing I learned is that vinegar in small bowls, opening windows, fans blowing, and candles burning all help. Praise God for Google! I now know that in a day or two, the house will be smelling great again. And baking some cookies will make it smell even better!

I woke up about 2:00 AM as I usually do, and this thought came to me. We all have our *Burned Macaroni* in our lives. Something that doesn't come easily or intuitively. Something we have to work on or we could make a big mistake. Possibly a costly mistake. For me, it is numbers and finances. I know that comes easily for some of you, but not for me. That is something I will always have to work on. Something made me laugh as I pondered all of this. I bet you are glad I didn't write a poem called *Burned Macaroni*.

Going deeper. Another thought that has surfaced from time to time is that if my husband goes to heaven before me, I am the one who will need to do the finances, and that scares me even though he has everything very organized for me. Again, for those of you who this comes easily, you are probably shaking your head. I know that if I

50

go to heaven first, my husband will learn (maybe by trial and error) how to cook. Or there are lots of great places for take-out. And of course, ice cream is very easy to fix!

No worries. I'm not planning on going to heaven anytime soon. Just the opposite. I plan to enjoy each day to the fullest with as much enthusiasm and energy and laughter than I can.

Here are a couple things that come easily for me. Prayer. Some of my most intense prayer times are from 2:00 AM to 5:00 AM. Yes, I know I am a head bobber around 7:30 or 8:00 PM (although occasionally I stay awake until ten or eleven!) There is an old hymn "Count Your Blessings, Name Them One By One." That is how I start out. Naming my blessings. . .each person in our family, the miracle that my husband and I have almost been married fifty years and we get to enjoy life as much as we do. The list of blessings goes on and on. Then there are specific prayer requests. Some confidential. Some that we are all praying for. Some very specific prayer requests. Angels of protection, healing, forgiveness, growth, faith, the struggles of life, the wonder of life.

I am so thankful my children and grandchildren are grounded in Jesus. Just yesterday, one grandchild said a Bible verse to me from memory. Last week another grandchild wanted to put something on the gratitude wall at church. She spoke and I wrote it down for her, "I love God because He loves me." I have heard precious words like that from each of the grandchildren. One time I was walking and holding hands with another grandchild. He turned to me and said, "Grandma, the most important thing is for everyone to love Jesus." Wow to all of these moments!

Another thing that comes easily for me is being a cheerleader. Not the high school or college kind! Besides, I don't jump very well and I definitely can't do the splits. I mean a day to day cheerleader. So here is my cheer for today! Let's enjoy today and savor the ride! Who knows, we may learn something very valuable. Just like I did with Burned Macaroni! Everyone makes mistakes. Everyone is good at something. Prayer is powerful!

Written Monday, November 27, 2017

"This is love: not that we loved God, but that he loved us and sent his Sone as an atoning sacrifice for our sins."
1 John 4:10

Cancer

I recognized the number
On my cell phone.
The doctor just told me
It's cancer they found.

I've heard this before,
This time more real.
The fear is gripping,
Terror is here.

I'm headed to heaven
One day that's for sure.
I just am not ready
For heaven right now.

I prayed, "Heal me, Jesus!"
And asked others to pray.
I felt His presence
With me day by day.

I recognized the number
On my cell phone.
The doctor just told me
The cancer is all gone!

Written June 27, 2018

I wrote this after my second encounter with cancer. This time it was melanoma. My heart goes out to any of you who are dealing with cancer right now.

"Have mercy on me, Lord, for I am faint;
heal me, Lord, for my bones are in agony."
Psalm 6:2

Cancer Survivor

I'm a cancer survivor,
Let the praises begin.
New life I've been given,
Each day a discovery,
Each moment a gem.

Sometimes I slip back,
To my unappreciative days,
Forgetting that this treasure,
Is merely made of clay.

Halleluiah—Praise God
I'm a cancer survivor!
Each day a discovery,
Each moment a gem!

Written February 2, 2010

I wrote this a few years after my first encounter with cancer.

*"Nevertheless, I will bring health and healing to it; I will heal my
people and will let them enjoy abundant peace and security."
Jeremiah 33:6*

Christmas Joy

Oh, Christmas joy,
This star lit night.
The gift from heaven,
A birth so bright!

Together we hold
Each other's hand,
Together we sing
Silent Night and stand.

One night alone
A Savior is given.
Our lives are changed,
Our souls have risen!

Oh, Christmas joy,
This star lit night.
The gift from heaven,
A birth so bright!

Thank you, God,
Thank you, Spirit,
Sweet Jesus is alive,
Let everyone hear it!

Oh, Christmas joy!

This poem doesn't have a date that I wrote it. Christmas joy is timeless!

"When they saw the star, they were overjoyed."
Matthew 2:10

Christmas Time

Another Christmas, another year.
It's a time for buying and baking
And enjoying the holiday cheer.
What a wonderful time of year!

I still remember when our family was two,
And now there are five!
Three special blessings—just to name a few.
This time in our lives is golden!

Sometimes I wish we could stay here forever,
Our little family of five.
But I know three who would say, "No way, Never!"
It isn't how life is meant to be.

So, this Christmas I will treasure
And I won't have any regrets.
I look to the future with pleasure
As I see our family grow.

And then there will only be you and me
And I'll treasure those Christmases,
Because as you can see,
I am with the only man for me!

Written to my husband on Christmas 1990.

*"An angel of the Lord appeared to them, and the glory of the Lord
shone around them, and they were terrified. But the angel said to
them, 'Do not be afraid. I bring you good news that will cause
great joy for all the people. Today in the town of David a Savior
has been born to you; he is the Messiah, the Lord.'"*
Luke 2:9-11

Confirmation Day

I looked at you today—so beautiful and fair,
Those sparkly eyes, that wavy, thick brown hair;
And deep inside a heart of gold.
You're the baby girl I used to hold.

And I will remember every day,
Those melodies you would play.
The way we laughed and cried
Together through life side by side.

I thank God for you
And I know this is true.
Our prayers were answered that day
When God sent you our way!

In our family confirmation day at church was another milestone in life. Time to reflect. Time to express their faith.

"And whatever you do, whether in word or deed,
do it all in the name of the Lord Jesus,
giving thanks to God the Father through him."
Colossians 3:17

Couple in Love

Hands entwined, hearts have crossed.
You are walking side by side,
A couple clearly in love.
It is impossible to hide.

Mirrored souls, yet not the same,
You quickly blended as one.
Time together—here and there,
Your lives are filled with fun.

God has set you on this path,
He will guide you every day.
Give your love to each other
And He will bless you in every way!

Written May 15, 2006 for a specific couple, although the words apply to any couple in love!

"And the two will become one flesh.
So they are no longer two, but one flesh.
Therefore what God has joined together, let no one separate."
Mark 10:8-9

Cuddle Time

It's such a little thing;
A cuddle here, a cuddle there.
A cuddle in the morning,
But they keep the fires burning.

A time to touch,
With words or not,
A time with tender meaning.
A time for each one leaning.

The breakfast of champs,
Not cereal and milk,
But I would simply say
Some cuddling every day!

Written June 20, 1988

*"Finally, brothers and sisters, whatever is true, whatever is noble,
whatever is right, whatever is pure, whatever is lovely,
whatever is admirable—if anything is excellent or praiseworthy—
think about such things."*
Philippians 4:8

Destined to Be Together!

Friends at first, then something more,
Their lives were meant to cross.
Time together. Time forever,
Only God could open that door!

Gazing at each other with lover's eyes,
Making up with that special touch.
Walking side by side with glowing pride,
Enjoying the moment. The time really flies!

The bride is beautiful with light brown hair,
Her smile lights up the room.
She turns to him,
There is love in the air!

The groom is handsome, tall, and strong.
His partner's hand in his,
They earnestly repeat their vows.
One Hand, One Heart is their wedding song.

Husband and wife from this day on,
They were destined to be together,
Laughing, growing, loving, praying,
Thanking God for all He has done!

Written June 5, 2004

*"Love is patient, love is kind. It does not envy, it does not boast, it
is not proud. It does not dishonor others, it is not self-seeking, it
is not easily angered, it keeps no record of wrongs. Love does not
delight in evil but rejoices with the truth. It always protects, always
trusts, always hopes, always perseveres."*
1 Corinthians 13:4-6

Do You Miss Your Tears?

When your heart is bursting
With happiness and pride,
Do you miss your tears?

When your heart is heavy
With hurt feelings and pain,
Do you miss your tears?

Tears of happiness,
Tears of joy,
Tears of sorrow,
Tears of fear,

Though they are on the inside,
May they wash upon your soul
And remind you of God's touch.
How He loves you so!

January 15, 2010

I wrote this poem after talking to someone who was on a medication that evened out her emotions so much that she couldn't cry even if she wanted to. She missed her tears.

*"Those who sow with tears
will reap with songs of joy."
Psalm 126:5*

Double Diamond Moments

What makes me smile in a minute
Are double diamond moments we share.
A ride in the convertible
With the wind blowing our hair.

What you mean to me is more than that,
Praying, learning, talking, laughing, crying.
"I have your back," you would say.
At times our spirits low, other times flying!

You taught me about the cross of Christ,
Seeing it in front of others,
It gives new light, new love, forgiveness,
And helps us be sisters and brothers.

Our "therapy" sessions have been a blast,
Each one has been divine.
Let each one be a surprise
So much fun every time!

Written January 8, 2010

The term double-diamond moments came from our pastor. He talked about how we often go around and around on the bunny hills of life. If we just step out, there are often double-diamond experiences waiting for us and a way to connect to people that we never dreamed of.

"Give, and it will be given to you. A good measure, pressed down, shaken together and running over, will be poured into your lap. For with the measure you use, it will be measured to you."
Luke 6:38

Each Day

Each day a new beginning,
Each day part of God's plan.
Each day some special beauty
Is waiting to be found!

Each day has a beginning,
It always has an end.
We live in the in-between,
Where our minds have already been!

I wrote this about the newness, the possibilities of each day!

"In the morning, Lord, you hear my voice;
in the morning I lay my requests before you
and wait expectantly."
Psalm 5:3

Each Day!

Each day is an adventure,
We wonder what's in store.
Someone new to meet?
God is always opening doors!

Rejoice in the morning,
Rejoice throughout the day,
Thank you, Jesus,
For leading the way!

And when the day is almost over,
Sitting quietly with your mind,
Bless each person from your thoughts,
Making every day more wonderful – the best kind!

Written March 29, 2007

*"Out of his fullness we have all received grace
in place of grace already given."*
John 1:16

Eagle Wings

To become an Eagle Scout is an accomplishment beyond compare;
They met the goal through hard work, honor, and pride.
An Eagle soars where others would not dare.

One day an elderly aunt was asked if she understood,
Her young relatives were changing from boys to Eagle Scout men.
She smiled and pointed to her hospital closet and her prized possession.

Upon a jacket that she wore daily with pride,
Was an Eagle pin her own son earned,
When he was young and stood by her side.

With that same emotion in our hearts,
We invite you to share this moment.
Growing, learning, helping, reaching,
It's not the end, it's the start!

Presented on Sunday, July 23, 2000

I was asked to write a poem for the invitation for two relatives who would be presented with their Eagle Wings. It was quite an accomplishment.

"In the same way, let your light shine before others, that they may see your good deeds and glorify your Father in heaven."
Mathew 5:16

EGR!

Is there someone who irritates you?
That person gets on your nerves,
A word here or a tone there,
The positive times are few!

We know the drill,
The right thing to do,
Forgive and forget,
Block your mind with your will!

I heard this saying long ago:
Extra Grace Required—EGR.
Say it over and over again,
It will calm you so!

EGR
EGR
EGR
Extra Grace Required!

Written December 30, 2009

Someone told me about the term EGR. Her pastor used the term in a sermon. It was such a great reminder that we need to have special grace for those EGR people in our lives!

"Bear with each other and forgive one another if any of you has a grievance against someone. Forgive as the Lord forgave you."
Colossians 3:13

Engaged!

April first is a special day.
The ring, the laughter, the dinner, the show,
So much fun in every way.
You're engaged! Let everyone know!

Soon you will be husband and wife,
Congratulations to you both!
God's blessings your entire life,
Your happiness lights the room!

Written April 1, 2011

"Rejoice in the Lord always. I will say it again: Rejoice!"
Philippians 4:4

Face of A Child

Sometimes we wonder what God
Has in store for the future,
And then we look into
The face of a child and know
That God continues to create,
God continues to bless,
God continues to live,
In the soul of a child!

Written May 3, 2009

*"Every good and perfect gift is from above, coming down from
the Father of the heavenly lights, who does not change like
shifting shadows."*
James 1:17

Fill the Void, Lord

Sometimes, when I'm feeling sad or lonely,
There's a prayer I tend to pray.
Fill the void, Lord, fill the void.

There might be people all around me,
Yet I'm lonely.
There might be a smile on my face.
Fill the void, Lord, fill the void.

It never fails to happen,
He always answers this simple prayer,
In ways that surprise me,
Through kindness from others,
Little by little
The void begins to fill!

I don't have a date on this one, but I know I wrote it a long time ago.
The words of the prayer are as true today and they were then.

*"Be strong and courageous. Do not be afraid or terrified because
of them, for the Lord your God goes with you; he will never leave
you nor forsake you."*
Deuteronomy 31:6

Fingertips Touching

Fingertips touching from birth to this day.
A mother and daughter bonded by love,
You are marrying your best friend,
And the privilege is mine
To hold your hand and say,
"May God bless you always!"

Written May 19, 2007

"And God is able to bless you abundantly,
so that in all things at all times, having all that you need,
you will abound in every good work."
2 Corinthians 9:8

First Day of School

You started school today
With enthusiasm and a smile on your face.
Moments ago, you were by my side,
In such a different place.

I'm proud of you,
How much you've grown
And learned about this world.
Seeds of wisdom are being sown.

Little by little I'm letting go.
It's not easy for me,
But I'm happy and a little sad,
All part of life—you will see!

Enjoy the journey!

Written August 27, 2012

Sending your child can be a big deal whether it is preschool or college!

"Jesus said, 'Let the little children come to me, and do not hinder them, for the kingdom of heaven belongs to such as these.'"
Matthew 19:14

For You

This poem is for you,
It's coming your way.
A word of encouragement,
Something funny or something
That pierces your heart.
I'm writing it just for you
Early today!

Written July 3, 2018 at 1:30 AM

I write many of my poems early in the morning. I wake up with words swirling in my head. I can't sleep so I might as well go write them down!

"Therefore encourage one another and build each other up,
just as in fact you are doing."
1 Thessalonians 5:11

From Different Lands

I know that I will often look,
Where you used to sit and draw,
Watch a movie or read a book,
And I'll remember a wonderful young man.

Our families live so far apart,
Likes and differences, there are so many.
I've loved having you here from the start
And hope you feel the same.

Someday, along the way,
Our lives are sure to cross.
And may we smile and say
We're friends from different lands!

Written August 25, 1994

We were fortunate to have a high school student from France live with us a short time one summer. What really was a blessing was connecting with him and his family quite a few years later. The last line of the poem is true!

"As iron sharpens iron,
so one person sharpens another."
Proverbs 27:17

From Thanksgiving to Christmas

He bowed his head
To say the grace
Some tears slid down
His saddened face,

For those departed
No longer here,
In heaven now
No pain, no fear.

For miracles wrought
And death defied,
For cancer free
Our mom abides.

For little ones
With starry eyes,
The love of life
And childlike cries.

We gather here,
Let Christmas ring.
Share some love,
Give thanks and sing!

This was written after my brother-in-law said a beautiful prayer at a family gathering.

> *"Look to the Lord and his strength;*
> *seek his face always."*
> *1 Chronicles 16:11*

Fruit of The Spirit

Love, joy, peace, forbearance, kindness, goodness, faithfulness, gentleness and self-control.

It's easy to look at others
And see what is missing,
But when I look within,
Others could say the same about me.

The fruits of the spirit are beautiful,
The fruits of the spirit are free,
I pray that each of these
Are truly growing in me.

Written on May 3, 2008

*"But the fruit of the Spirit is love, joy, peace, forbearance,
kindness, goodness, faithfulness, gentleness and self-control.
Against such things there is no law."
Galatians 5:22-23*

Gift of Love

Snowflakes falling out our window
Or twinkling stars on a warm summer night.
Everyday moments remind me of you,
The man I love who holds me tight!

Wonder in the gift of love,
A union beyond compare,
Time to grow and time to learn,
What a God-given bond we share!

Years have flown, that's for sure.
Thirty-five years together this spring,
"A couple in love," they say.
You're my friend, my love, my everything!

I had dreamed that one day my husband and I would take a trip to France. I was amazed when it happened! My husband and I celebrated our thirty-fifth anniversary in Paris on a dinner cruise down the Seine. I was so touched by the moment that I was in tears most of the evening. Happy tears.

> *"Place me like a seal over your heart,*
> *like a seal on your arm;*
> *for love is as strong as death,*
> *its jealousy unyielding as the grave.*
> *It burns like blazing fire,*
> *like a mighty flame."*
> *Song of Songs 8:6*

God Has Provided

God has provided in so many ways,
Sunshine, happiness, joy in my soul,
Answered prayers and spirit-filled days,
Thank you, Jesus, my best friend!

Direction for the path of life
Is my daily prayer.
No more worry and needless strife,
Your wisdom leads me on!

God's gifts are real and true,
Faith, family, friends and life,
Just to name a few,
Thank you, thank you Jesus!

God has provided!

Written on March 3, 2009

"Thanks be to God for his indescribable gift!"
2 Corinthians 9:15

God's Hand

He tapped me on the shoulder
And softly said my name,
Let's walk this way a while,
Your life won't ever be the same.
And so I put my hand in His,
And let Him lead the way.
The doubts have bombarded me,
But He's there day after day.
I don't know where He's leading me
But I know I'll hold His hand.
As God leads me—oh so tenderly,
Wherever I go, He's holding my hand!

This poem was written on March 6, 1992 when I was looking for a teaching job. I had stayed home with our three children for a mere sixteen years, and I was ready and wanting to get back into teaching. The search was frustrating and discouraging. I couldn't understand how I could have such a burning desire to be back in the classroom and not find a position that worked for me. I was a French major, and I kept getting offers to teach Spanish. Even when I bluntly said I don't speak Spanish, this was the response, "You'll learn it!" I didn't realize it at the time, but God was leading me to a corporation, and I would go on to be an officer in the company over Corporate Training and led a team of sixteen talented, smart trainers! Is God leading you to something and gently saying, "Just hold my hand?" You can do it!

"Show me your ways, Lord,
teach me your paths.
Guide me in your truth and teach me,
for you are God my Savior,
and my hope is in you all day long."
Psalm 25:4-5

79

Going Home

I'm going home.
My soul is soaring,
Focus on praising,
Not on the pain.
I thought it would be different,
But that's not true,
I'm going home.

I was really looking forward to a great Thanksgiving with our family.
Instead, I got very sick, and we had to travel three hours to get home.
Going home could have lots of meanings.

"Have no fear of sudden disaster
or of the ruin that overtakes the wicked,
for the Lord will be at your side
and will keep your foot from being snared."
Proverbs 3:25-26

Golden Thread

Golden thread
Encircling three,
Hearts together,
Sisters forever.

I see the golden thread
Connecting our friendship of three.
God granting this miraculous bonding
That only He could see.

It started slowly, the little thread
And then began to spread.
Tighter, tighter, the pattern is woven
By His hand the loom is led.

My sisters you have given
Much more than I can repay,
I'll just thank God for our friendship
In this simple way.

Written June 30, 1988

Over the years I have been blessed with friendships of three. I am amazed how God brings these friendships together, and I am so thankful for them!

> *"My command is this: Love each other as I have loved you.*
> *Greater love has no one than this: to lay down one's life for*
> *one's friends."*
> *John 15:12-13*

Graduation Day

The time has come
For you to wear a cap and gown.
Your college days are complete,
It's a new path you'll walk down!

It wasn't that long ago
When you said which college was your plan.
We replied, "How far is that?"
"Think about one closer, if you can!"

Friends from so many places,
A journey abroad and beyond.
An education to shape your world,
Even with professors you formed a bond!

To say we are proud
And love you so,
The words are simple and sweet,
Like chocolate chips or an ice cream treat!

To another city you say?
That sounds good to us,
We can be right there
By car, by plane or bus!

We won't be far wherever you go,
God gave us such a beautiful gift.
You are our wonderful daughter,
Our prayers of thanks we lift!

Written May 9, 2004

"You will keep in perfect peace those whose minds are steadfast,
because they trust in you."
Isaiah 26:3

Grandpa Ralph

You met us with a smile
And said, "Glad to meet you."
We watched you sign with ease
While we struggled with <u>how</u> and <u>who</u>.

Just by being in your home
We had a small taste
Of a soundless world,
Our time was not a waste.

There was a machine for the phone
And a bell with a light,
Fast signing to watch
And captioned TV, isn't that right?

Long after I've forgotten words for my hands,
I'll remember a kind old man,
Who represented the need to care
For all the deaf in this land.

Written June 29, 1989

I took a sign language class, and the last class was going to someone's home who was deaf. The person we met was Grandpa Ralph, and we learned so much from him.

*"May the Lord now show you kindness and faithfulness, and I too
will show you the same favor because you have done this."
2 Samuel 2:6*

Happy Father's Day

In the garden of life, you have tended well,
The things put in your care.
More than lettuce, potatoes, and peas;
Your human touch is truly rare!

A smile, a laugh, a caring word,
Another brisket to cook.
You do it all with a giving heart.
Your life is an open book!

Happy Father's Day, dad!
The words are hard to find.
The message from your Garden Crop,
"You are one of a kind!"

I wrote this to my dad. He loved to garden, and he loved people.
What a great combination!

> *"I made gardens and parks and*
> *planted all kinds of fruit trees in them."*
> *Ecclesiastes 2:5*

Happy First Days of Summer

May ice cream dribble down your chin,
May happiness come from deep within,
May your golf shots be straight and true,
May you have soft breezes and skies of blue,
May you splash in a pool with childlike glee,
May you feel completely free,
May you walk slowly on starlit nights,
May your summer be out of sight!

Written June 21, 2004

"Take delight in the Lord,
and he will give you the desires of your heart."
Psalm 37:4

Happy Valentine's Day

I love you in the morning,
I love you in the night,
I love you when we're far apart,
Or when you squeeze me tight.

Today is another day,
A gift we've been given.
I love the things we do each day,
And the life we are livin'

You're a Valentine of a Lifetime,
A love by my side.
I treasure the journey we are on
It has been quite a ride!

Written February 14, 2007

"And over all these virtues put on love,
which binds them all together in perfect unity.
Colossians 3:14"

He Died For Me

What if I was the only one
Who walked upon this earth?
The outcome would be the same,
He would die for little me!

My sins alone are enough,
To nail Him to the cross.
He didn't falter or hesitate,
His love is overflowing!

Not only did He die for me
He conquered death as well.
He rose that Easter morning,
So, I will live for eternity!

Written after a Bible study on April 7, 2009. We talked about the
personal meaning of Holy Week for each of us.

"I have been crucified with Christ and I no longer live, but Christ
lives in me. The life I now live in the body, I live by faith in the Son
of God, who loved me and gave himself for me."
Galatians 2:20

He Heals

I was on my knees this morning
With a very thankful heart.
After waking with a jolt and
A direct word from God.

He helped you driving home
With His tender loving care,
Then heard our fervent prayers
To bring healing from within.

We watched a miracle take place
It was right before our eyes.
He touched your very soul
And is bringing healing to your face!

Written May 3, 2008
2:00 AM

This poem was for someone who was suffering from an infection that had settled in her face. Her face was swollen, and she was in pain. The big issue was that she was leaving in a few days on a once in a lifetime trip. God really wants us to pray about everything!

"Do not be anxious about anything, but in every situation, by prayer and petition, with thanksgiving, present your requests to God. And the peace of God, which transcends all understanding, will guard your hearts and your minds in Christ Jesus."
Philippians 4:6-7

Heart of Gold

Heart of gold,
Caring soul for those in need.
Smiles and tears freely given,
Quietly serving others.
The hands and feet of God,
An angel in our midst.

That is who you are
To me and so many more.
God has given you
That special touch.

Your work on earth
Is often hard,
Requiring super-human strength.
Things are thrown at you,
Bumps along the path.
Humbly you bow
And ask for God's plan.

As your forever friend,
I am truly blessed.
To laugh and cry and pray with you,
An angel in our midst!

Written May 13, 2015

"Because I love your commands
more than gold, more than pure gold,"
Psalm 119:127

Heavenly Babe

Oh, heavenly Babe in the Virgin's arms
What a wonder to me you are.
My heart wants to bend, to reach, to touch,
But so often I look from afar.

Oh, heavenly Babe in the Virgin's arms
Is there sadness in your eyes?
To think that Your life must pay
For my sins and unbelieving lies.

Oh, Jesus Christ in Mary's arms,
Thank you for coming this way.
So precious, so small, so humble–
Help me to grow more like you day by day!

"For to us a child is born,
to us a son is given,
and the government will be on his shoulders.
And he will be called
Wonderful Counselor, Mighty God,
Everlasting Father, Prince of Peace."
Isaiah 9:6

Here for You

Sometimes when we're together
The words just seem to flow
And other times when words are few,
We both just seem to know.

I'm here for you, you're here for me.
Each other's one and only mate.
What brought us together so long ago?
I guess it must be fate.

One of my favorite times
Is cuddling close to you,
I'm here for you, you're here for me.
We're saying, "I love you too!"

You will notice quite a few love poems to my husband. At first, I would give them to him and practically run out of the room. Now, I am brave enough to write them in cards or even frame some of them and read the words face to face. Maybe someone in your life is waiting for you to read one of these poems to him or her!

"And let us consider how we may spur one another
on toward love and good deeds."
Hebrews 10:24

Hope

Fall-time coloring,
Brilliant oranges and red.
Such a vibrant time
Before the season's end.

Much to my surprise,
Two lovely purple irises
Proudly showed their beauty.
A sign of HOPE
Is what they meant to me!

Written October 20, 2010

A few years ago I was given some iris bulbs from my mother-in-law's garden. She had passed away several years ago, but one of her children kept the irises going in her yard. I forgot about them for some time so the bulbs sat in a sack in my garage. Last fall I decided to plant them to see if we would have flowers this spring. The plants grew, but there were no blooms. Then yesterday in the full swing of fall, I saw two beautiful irises. It was like a sign from God saying He can do anything. Hold onto that as you go through the hard times. Have hope!

> *"But those who hope in the Lord*
> *will renew their strength.*
> *They will soar on wings like eagles;*
> *they will run and not grow weary,*
> *they will walk and not be faint."*
> *Isaiah 40:31*

Hope Begins

Piercing pain, troubled souls,
Lies, anger, physical burdens,
With no end in sight.
Little by little, spirits found,
Pain was shared to help subside.

It doesn't completely disappear
But in the moment of sharing
And the amazing power of God
Light appears, hope begins,
Whatever the future holds.

Written January 18, 2012

"God is our refuge and strength, an ever-present help in trouble."
Psalm 46:1

Hope Renewed

Hope returning, hope renewed,
To discover each day
And what it brings.
Gifts of sunshine and friendship,
Emotions up and down,
Hope returning, hope renewed.

Lord, help me see
Open my eyes,
Give my heart
Permission to feel.
Hope returning, hope renewed.

Sometimes I am discouraged,
Sometimes I am sad all day.
Gently move me forward,
To hope coming my way!
Hope returning, hope renewed!

Written February 9, 2012

Written for someone who said she needed hope!

*"He who was seated on the throne said, 'I am making everything
new!' Then he said, 'Write this down for these words are
trustworthy and true.'"*
Revelation 21:5

How Did You Know?

That your smiles would light my day,
That your gifts would touch my heart,
That your thoughts would make me whole?

I believe our lives crossed for a reason
And to me it's perfectly clear,
Whether we're together for just a season
Or maybe for many years.

No matter what time may give us,
I'll say it again with a smile,
Thank you for all you've given.
My new desk with be "in style!"

Written May 6, 1999

I wrote this poem to a group of people I had just trained. They showered me with gifts. I wanted them to know that they brightened my days!

*"And whatever you do, whether in word or deed, do it all in the
name of the Lord Jesus, giving thanks to
God the Father through him."*
Colossians 3:17

I Dare

Sometimes we are stressed,
Too exhausted to think.
The kids are fighting,
Dirty dishes in the sink.

Our minds are full
Of issues from work,
It's not our problem
Everyone else is a jerk.

We grumble and complain
That life is not fair,
We are angry and unhappy,
Our days falling into despair.

I dare us to stop believing those lies,
To fall on our knees and pour out our hearts.
Open God's Word and mediate on a verse,
Our new life for God is ready to start!

The bumps in the road,
Rainbows and sunshine,
Are beyond our wisdom and comprehension.
God's in control and it's totally fine!

God, fill us with joy
And a wonder of life,
With minds full of praise
And words without strife!

Grant us that rest
And renewal of our minds,
May we live for Your glory.
On fire Christians—the best kind!

Written January 25, 2008 in the middle of the night.

"Come to me, all you who are weary and burdened,
and I will give you rest."
Matthew 11:28

I Didn't See That Coming

"I didn't see that coming!"
It came out of the blue
An insult, harsh words, or a complete attack,
What is a person to do?

Give it back with equal fire?
Something hurtful and quick?
No, that's not the way,
Causing heartache and making yourself sick.

If you can, smile and simply say,
"I didn't see that coming!"
You'll relax and maybe laugh
And the schemes of the devil will go running!

Written October 9, 2012

*"Do not repay evil with evil or insult with insult. On the contrary,
repay evil with blessing, because to this you were called so that
you may inherit a blessing."*
1 Peter 3:9

I Give You My Heart

I remember. . .
When we first said, "I love you!"
We were young, and our worries were few,
I gave you my heart!

Since then our path has been clear
To walk hand in hand,
The engagement, then becoming husband and wife,
Daily joys can be Happy Land,
Because I gave you my heart!

As a man, you can walk tall
With integrity within and God as your guide.
A tender heart, a loving spirit
For forever, I want you by my side,
I give you my heart always!

Written February 14, 2004

"Do everything in love."
1 Corinthians 16:14

I Pray

May God with His POWER
Protect you this way.
From the very beginning
To the end of each day!

May God with His LOVE
Give you kindness to others.
Those along your path,
Your sisters and brothers!

May God with His WISDOM
Give you talents to share.
The world is brighter
Because you are there!

May God with His PLAN
In Jesus His Son,
Guide you to heaven.
He's the One and only One!

Written on July 25, 2018

I originally wrote this to give to my grandchildren. Then I realized the words in the poem can apply to all of us, so I e-mailed it to many people. A friend and neighbor took this poem and created beautiful bookmarks. That amazed me and filled me with joy!

"God is mighty, but despises no one;
he is mighty, and firm in his purpose."
Job 36:5

I Remember

Warm cupcakes in the apple tree,
Money by my plate for the ice cream man,
Playing with dolls I thought were real,
Having a wonderful childhood.

Growing up you were there
At every event and occasion,
Giving, sewing, cooking,
I probably took you for granted.

Then I had children of my own,
I saw through a mother's heart,
We give and give and give some more,
It is how we show our love.

Thank you, mom for all you have done,
How you are still beside me,
Life is a journey—I want you to know,
I am blessed to have you for my Mom!

My mom loved the idea of giving us cupcakes when they were warm. My sister and I would be climbing in the apple tree in our back yard, and my mom brought out the cupcakes. Wonderful! She and my dad were great examples of supportive parents. Not perfect, but I have great memories.

"Every good and perfect gift is from above, coming down from the Father of the heavenly lights, who does not change like shifting shadows."
James 1:17

I Thought

I thought I needed peace
And received a storm instead.

I thought I needed patience
But my world fell apart.

I thought I needed comfort
But others turned to me for that.

I knew I needed wisdom
And God gave me His word.

Peace that passes understanding
And patience from above,
Comforting arms with an undying love.

Putting God first is so simple to do,
He really means it when He says,
"I am the only way!"
So richly does He bless us every day!

Written early in the morning on January 14, 2008.

"And the peace of God, which surpasses all understanding,
will guard your hearts and your minds in Christ Jesus."
Philippians 4:7

I Was Just Wondering Lord

Sometimes I look around and question where I am.
Giving here, giving there, and running in between.
Does my life really fit into Your great plan?
I was just wondering, Lord.

So many seem so confident with career and life
And here I am struggling—often alone.
Is that your only goal for me—a mother and wife?
I was just wondering, Lord.

Then I think how awesome your power alone can be,
Added to compassion Divine and simple love for man.
Will Your majesty truly set me free?
I was just wondering, Lord.

Can You help me see beyond the goals from day to day?
I seem so blind—could You make it clear?
Can You make me see my life in Your special way?
I was just wondering, Lord.

Written June 28, 1989

I think so many people wonder if they are doing what they truly
were meant to do.

"'For I know the plans I have for you,' declares the Lord,
'plans to prosper you and not to harm you, plans to give you
hope and a future.'"
Jeremiah 29:11

I'll Always Remember

I'll always remember . . .
How handsome you looked today,
Funny thing you would do and say,
What a gentle spirit is inside of you,
How days with you are so few.

Long before, from heaven you came,
In my heart was that special name —
Your name means "Gift from God" as you know,
It's a book in the Bible — your sister told you so!

Tall and bright and oh so strong,
In our hearts will always belong,
A precious place for those memories to store,
Of our son — whom we adore!

Written May 9, 1993

> *"I have no greater joy than to hear that my children*
> *are walking in the truth."*
> *3 John 4*

I'm A Flower

A tiny bud, closed and firm,
Just looking at the world,
Sometimes it drooped, sometime erect,
And slowly it unfurled.

A petal here, a petal there,
Each one has had some meaning.
I feel as though it's blossoming
But the process happens slowly.

A flower—for other to share,
Its meaning and its beauty.
A flower—growing and changing,
And sometimes fading.

But a flower never ending.

Written June 20, 1988

"And why do you worry about clothes? See how the flowers of the field grow. They do not labor or spin. Yet I tell you that not even Solomon in all his splendor was dressed like one of these."
Matthew 6:28-29

I'm a People Pleaser

I'm a people pleaser.
I have known it for years.
It's a problem,
Often causing tears.

Somehow, I think
Everyone must like me
If I'm just nice enough,
That's how it will be.

My feelings get hurt,
A very sensitive gal,
A word here—a tone there,
I'm sure they don't want to be my pal.

If I just think it through
Sometimes it makes me laugh.
They are just being themselves
And not giving me wrath.

This is a problem
I have to admit,
Taking others too seriously
My life in the pits.

The focus is then,
Totally on me.
It is not very Christ-like
That is easy to see.

I have verses ready,
When people pleasing comes along.
I'll read these verses carefully
And sing a Christian song.

We all have our weaknesses
I realize that now,
That's why we need Jesus,
Humbly to Him we bow!

Is this one of your weaknesses too? I think there are a lot of us.

"Bear with each other and forgive one another if any of you has a grievance against someone. Forgive as the Lord forgave you."
Colossians 3:13

I'm Addicted

I'm not a baby!
I just turned one!
I'm addicted to my bottle!
My bottle is so much fun!

I love my bottle!
It's comfort you see!
As long as Mom and Dad
Give it to me!

I hear them whispering,
"The time is here!
He has to give up
His bottle without fear!"

Okay, I'll try,
It's not easy at all,
To give up my bottle
And go play with a ball!

If you are addicted
To a bottle, a blanket or a toy,
Take my advice and
"Run!" says this one year old boy!

Written July 2, 2018

Written for a precious one-year-old child! The parents told me the child refuses to give up the bottle. They suggested I write a poem or children's story about it. That is what I did!

> *"He will yet fill your mouth with laughter*
> *and your lips with shouts of joy."*
> *Job 8:21*

I'm Back

There's a smile upon my face
And the fear is almost gone.
After I realized a decision
For me was entirely wrong.

There is an old expression
That for me is very true,
After it is gone forever,
We appreciate what we used to do.

I feel extremely fortunate,
God gave me back my life.
Once again confident,
As worker, mother, wife.

I will be forever grateful,
God loves me—it's a fact.
Family and friends stood beside me,
It was prayer that brought me back!

Written August 7 1994

I made a decision to leave a career path and go down another path.
I quickly realized that I had made a mistake. It was humbling to
admit, but I knew it was right for me to go back to the original career
path. I was so thankful!

"Give thanks in all circumstances;
for this is God's will for you in Christ Jesus."
1 Thessalonians 5:18

I'm Confident . . . I Think

To find the path, to listen to His voice
Is often so hard to do,
The path is not always clear.
Each step of the way
Sometimes I'm so sure and then doubt creeps in.
There is one thing I fear—
What if I look back and see clearly then,
That I was so wrong, and I can't take it back?

What made me this way? A fragile little bird,
Soaring one moment and crashing the next.
Lord, show me Your way
It's Your will I pray!

Written July 1993

*"Do not conform to the pattern of this world but be transformed
by the renewing of your mind. Then you will be able to test and
approve what God's will is—his good, pleasing and perfect will."*
Romans 12:2

I'm Obsessed!

They say it's melanoma
And now I am obsessed,
Cover myself with clothing,
What is the UPF?

First, I start with lotion.
Sunscreen is next,
SPF of thirty!
Or is fifty-five the best?

Make sure I use lots,
Then sunscreen clothes.
Pants, jacket, and hat,
Sunglasses are a must!

If I were to describe me,
This is the closest I can get.
I'm a beekeeper in hiding,
Those rays won't get me now!

Written June 27, 2018

This is a humorous look at the changes I made after a diagnosis of melanoma. Later, I wrote the words for the children's book The Beekeeper and The Turtle because that's what my husband and I looked like on our walks around the neighborhood. I was covered in sunscreen clothes, and he wore a back brace that looked like a turtle.

"Not only so, but we also glory in our sufferings, because we know that suffering produces perseverance; perseverance, character; and character, hope."
Romans 5:3-4

In My Heart, By My Side

Looking back. . .We were so excited when you were born.
Our third and last brought home with Christmas joy.
Met by a brother and sister who smiled with glee,
Because in you God had given them the best toy.

You were lively and full of spunk,
Extremely strong-willed and often balked
When I would take you from Miss Mona.
It was hard to believe you were three before you talked.

Cherished memories of those early years,
There is one that brings a tear.
We would hold hands and lie down for a nap,
Smiling, loving, bonding. . .it was great to have you near,
In my heart, by my side,

There was so much to do and not enough time.
Soccer, friends, plays at school, activities galore.
Who would guess that in your senior year
It was golf that you would adore.

This day is finally here,
A cap, a gown, a diploma in your hand.
The world is waiting for you to explore,
Your circle of friends will cover a wider band.

God be with you our daughter, with the outside voice,
Meet each day with wonder in the miracle of life
And always stay close to God
In the good times and the days of strife.

You will always be. . .
In our hearts, by our side!

Written May 28, 2000

"The Lord himself goes before you and will be with you;
he will never leave you nor forsake you. Do not be afraid;
do not be discouraged."
Deuteronomy 3:18

Is This The Day

Is this the day we hold our baby in our arms?
I wake up each morning with this thought on my mind.
Closer and closer we come to our special day,
Is this really happening?

Yes, very soon, our child will be in our arms,
Our emotions, probably a mixture of laughter and tears.
This miracle is happening all over the world
But when it's our home, it's a miracle beyond compare.

People are praying—there's a blanket of care.
When the time comes, our goal is clear,
Soon, very soon, we will hold our baby in our arms.
Is this the day?

Written March 23, 2009

"Jesus said, 'Let the little children come to me, and do not hinder them, for the kingdom of heaven belongs to such as these.'"
Matthew 19:14

It Doesn't Matter

I tell myself it doesn't matter
Whether I'm a teacher or I'm not.
Three times I thought He called to me
And His wisdom I sought.

Part of me that was a flame,
Soon became a burning fire.
To represent Him in the classroom
Was my heartfelt desire.

The picture of the classes
Was vivid in my mind.
My mind poured out new ideas,
An inspired teacher—the best kind.

But no was the answer I received,
The fire began to die.
Someday He will fulfill this dream
Or show me the reason why.

I can't let go of this dream,
It's burned upon my soul.
Oh God, let me know
That without it I am still whole!

Written May 4, 1988

I had been a stay at home mom for a long time, and then I had a burning desire to be back in the classroom. It was a longer and tougher journey than I expected. I ended up in a classroom in the corporate world!

"Hope deferred makes the heart sick,
but a longing fulfilled is a tree of life."
Proverbs 13:12

It's a Jungle Out There

From early in the morning
Until late at night
I'm working in the jungle
And it's always a fight—

Will I be the first to spear?
And will I get my prey?
If I turn my back
Will someone steal my goods away?

Yes—it's a jungle out there
And daily I must go
To care for my loved ones
It's not easy though.

Are you in the jungle of work right now? I wrote this poem for that
perspective.

"Whatever you do, work at it with all your heart,
as working for the Lord, not for human masters."
Colossians 3:23

It's Graduation

You walk across the stage with a diploma in your hand.
We smile and think what this day really means.
Yesterday you were only a child of three or four,
You would sing with a microphone and dance and twirl for hours,
You were wide-eyed and innocent, and we couldn't love you more!

Then there were grade school days with your best friend;
Laughing, growing, sharing—those times flew by so fast.
Before we knew it, junior high and high school were here.
A golden heart with graceful hands would glide over the keys
And music filled the house with beauty that brought a tear!

Four years seems so long ago when we talked about this day.
Underneath the oaks on Mother's Day, we would gather family round.
We pictured it in our minds, but it's reality now.
A daughter with a 4.0 and honors on and on,
We stand and clap and say, "Take a bow!"

Written May 13, 2001

Graduation from college is a big thing. However, the celebration is usually very subdued. I wanted our daughter to know we were so proud of her and all her hard work.

"Now then, stand still and see this great thing the
Lord is about to do before your eyes!"
1 Samuel 12:16

It's In Your Voice

I heard it in your voice today
And not in the usual way.
It was love I heard
And love I felt
And I heard it just today.

Can you fall in love again and again?
I'm here with a resounding yes.
Who in the world would guess?
I'd fall in love while singing a hymn,
It happened to me and I say, "Amen!"

God gave you a beautiful voice
And a love to sing out loud.
I'm glad God opened my ears today
To love you in another special way!

February 25, 1990

My husband has a wonderful voice, and I enjoy hearing him sing especially in church. For some reason this Sunday, I noticed his voice more than usual. Strong, deep tones filled with sincerity. I loved it all, and I loved him even more!

> *"The Lord bless you and keep you;*
> *the Lord make his face shine on you*
> *and be gracious to you;"*
> *Numbers 6:24-25*

Jim

He was a quiet man with a twinkle in his eyes;
Soft-spoken with a gentle soul.
Amazing strength in spite of declining health,
Discovered a skill in his golden years.
A beautiful Victorian doll house,
A masterpiece from his hands,
Filled with love for an adoring child,
Great grandchildren will treasure that for years!

Listening to sports, fishing with his grandson,
Spending time with family,
A few things he loved to do.

Memories left behind
To carry in your heart,
Of this quiet man with a twinkle in his eyes.
Lots of love for Jim!

Are there special older people in your life? It's wonderful to take time to appreciate all that they are and to treasure those memories after they are gone.

"He will wipe every tear from their eyes. There will be no more death or mourning or crying or pain, for the old order of things has passed away."
Revelation 21:4

John 3:16

I don't know why
This is happening to you.
I don't have the answers
For the timing of it all.

I do know this:
Today you are on the brink,
Eternity is on the other side.
God wants you to know for certain,
Jesus wants to be your guide.

There is a verse
That says it all.
John 3:16—This is how it goes:
"For God so loved the world
That He gave His one and only Son,
That whoever believes in Him shall not perish
But have eternal life."

May you have peace and comfort
As you cross to heaven's side.
Eternal life is yours to have,
Believing in God's son

Written January 21, 2010

There are people in your life who are on the brink. They may be on the brink of death, the brink of accepting Jesus, the brink of despair, or the brink of heaven. I wrote these words when I was desperately trying to share God's love and eternity, before it was too late. May God's Spirit keep you strong to share wherever and whenever you can.

"For God so loved the world that he gave his one and only Son, that whoever believes in him shall not perish but have eternal life."
John 3:16

Jonah Learned to Obey

One day Johan heard God say—
"Go to Nineveh and tell the people
To stop what they're doing and turn to Me."
But Jonah was afraid and turned away.
Yes, Jonah didn't obey, and he turned away.

He got on a boat going the other way
And thought his problem was over.
But a storm almost took their lives
Because Jonah was afraid and turned away,
Because Jonah didn't obey, and he turned away.

So, they threw him over the ship that day
And inside a big fish he landed.
For three days he was there,
Scared at first, but at last he prayed,
"I'm still afraid, but I want to obey.
Yes, I want to obey today!"

So, let's learn from Jonah and obey.
Yes, God will show us the way,
Don't turn away, learn to obey!

Written on May 16, 1990

I taught a group of second grade students at our church. We had just studied the story about Jonah. I wrote this poem so they could act out the story for a closing program at the end of the year. Our youngest daughter read the poem, and the other students acted it out. It made the story come to life for them!

"Then the word of the Lord came to Jonah a second time:
'Go to the great city of Nineveh and
proclaim to it the message I give you.'"
Jonah 3:1-2

Legacy

This last week we have had weddings,
We have had funerals,
There have been tremendous joys, and even silly times,
And deep sorrow,
In all of these events, one of life's lessons appears.
We decide what kind of legacy we leave behind,
That legacy is shaped not by what life gives us
But by what we give to life.

*"Love the Lord your God with all your heart and with all your soul
and with all your strength. These commandments that I give you
today are to be on your hearts. Impress them on your children. Talk
about them when you sit at home and when you walk along the
road, when you lie down and when you get up."*
Deuteronomy 6:5-7

Let's Finish Strong

Today is the start
Of each day together.
Let's finish strong
And make the best of it.
A life according to God's plan,
Let's finish strong!

It dawned on me that my husband and I have the potential of making this last part of our time together the strongest ever. This would definitely have a strong, positive effect on our love and marriage, but also a strong and living legacy for our children and grandchildren.

"We love because he first loved us."
1 John 4:19

Letter from God

I look at you my child
And see what I have made.
The child before,
The person now,
The adult soon to be.
I see your heart
And I know when you are hurting.
Believe me when I say this:
My love will never sway,
I loved you as a little child,
I love you so today.
And each of your tomorrows,
I will love you day-by-day.
So, when doubt and uncertainty
Creep in your mind today,
Tell satan, God made you special
And you are His always!

Love,
Your Heavenly Father

Written September 18, 1988

I wrote this thinking what it would be like if God wrote a letter to us.
In this poem I was thinking about a particular person, but this could
apply to anyone!

> *"But God demonstrates his own love for us in this:*
> *While we were still sinners, Christ died for us."*
> *Romans 5:8*

Letter to God

Sometimes I think if I look hard enough,
He'll come walking through the door.
That old familiar smile, the look, the hug,
I know he won't be gone long.
Carry me through this, carry me through.

I went to his closet, that old familiar smell.
The memories rush over me,
I want them to be real.
Oh God, this can't be happening.
Carry me through this, carry me through.

Your people have surrounded me
With hugs, love and tears.
The food appears before us
And I know that You are here.
Carry me through this, carry me through.

This poem is written to anyone who has lost a loved one. This was
written for a particular person. I even wrote it before I realized this
friend was having a hard day. I pray this will touch those of you who
are hurting from the loss of a loved one.

"When I was in distress, I sought the Lord;
at night I stretched out untiring hands,
and I would not be comforted."
Ecclesiastics 3:1-4

Life is Not a Mystery

I know this sounds strange,
I know it sounds odd,
Life is not a mystery,
When we live it for God!

He is taller than mountains,
Wider than the sea,
Here before time began
And created you and me!

Take time to ponder,
Take time to pray,
God wants our passion,
For life every day!

We want answers—we want them now.
This life will not magically fall from the sky,
As we trudge through each day without any joy,
For sure it won't come when we're always asking—Why?

Realize each minute is a gift from God.
How we spend it is ours to give,
It will only have meaning,
When it's for God we live!

I know this sounds strange,
I know it sounds odd,
Life is not a mystery,
When we live it for God!

Written January 25, 2008 in the middle of the night

"For from him and through him and for him are all things.
To him be the glory forever! Amen."
Romans 11:36

Light In The Darkness

I sat alone in the dark,
My thoughts, my only companion.
Sadness surrounded me,
A wall of despair.

Then suddenly it changed,
Light entered the room.
I felt a presence there.
A glimmer of hope,
An answer to unspoken prayer.
Light in the darkness,
Light in the darkness!

Written July 16, 2013

When we hit a wall, sometimes we sit in the darkness. And at the right time, God reveals His light, His presence, and His hope.

> *"Your word is a lamp for my feet,*
> *a light on my path."*
> *Psalm 119:105*

Lonely

Surrounded by people
I still feel alone.
There is noise and laughter
But for me there is none.

Yesterday was bright,
Today is gloomy and dark.
Will this cloud lift,
So I can see the stars?

I need to reach out,
Not sure who to call.
Will they hear I am lonely?
Or hear nothing at all?

There is hope in the future.
A plan meant for me.
Step by step,
I will follow His lead!

Written June 27, 2018 for people who are feeling lonely.

"He will call on me, and I will answer him;
I will be with him in trouble,
I will deliver him and honor him."
Psalm 91:15

Love to Last A Lifetime

Love to last a lifetime,
Love that's meant to last.
Love where the future
Is stronger than the past.

Thirty-five years together,
My love, friend, and mate.
I know our time together
Is more than simply fate.

God designed a purpose,
We're part of that Heavenly plan.
One Hand, One Heart,
Is how it all began!

*"Three things will last forever—faith, hope, and love—and
the greatest of these is love."
1 Corinthians 13:3*

Loved by You

I'm weary, there's aching in my bones.
I'm tired of all this mess,
I'm tired of being alone.
I need Strength and Guidance.

Who understands my pain?
Who can help me through it?
There is sunshine, but lots of rain,
Cloudy skies, but blue horizons.

At time these feelings are intense
And bring me to my knees.
When I look up, it starts to make sense,
I know the Author of Peace.

An encouraging word here, a laugh there,
A baby in my arms, a friend across the miles.
So many give and so many share,
These gifts are priceless, of this I am sure.

God, guide me night and day,
Calm me and settle my thoughts.
Help me remember in little ways
That I am special and loved by You!

Written December 16, 2008

"A cheerful heart is good medicine,
but a crushed spirit dries up the bones."
Proverbs 17:22

Meant To Be

Two hearts met not long ago,
A mirror image—clear to some
But not to those involved.
You were meant to be as one!

Down career paths you walked,
God provided interesting twists,
Side by side friends you became.
Who would guess one day you'd kiss!

Your love divinely given,
Your lives forever bound,
Husband and wife from this day forward.
A gift that's sought and now is found!

May God surround you with His majesty
Today and all your tomorrows!

Written for people I worked with who fell in love.

*"Yours, Lord, is the greatness and the power
and the glory and the majesty and the splendor,
for everything in heaven and earth is yours.
Yours, Lord, is the kingdom;
you are exalted as head over all."*
1 Chronicles 29:11

Miracle of Miracles

Miracle of miracles,
God has brought you to this place.
You are so in love,
It shows clearly on your face.

Husband and wife from this day forward,
To have and to hold forever and ever.
Side by side through good times and hard ones,
Someone to encourage you, whatever you endeavor.

This day is wonderful, your joy is alive.
You are so beautiful as the bride,
A gown of ivory and sparkles in your eyes.
The handsome groom smiling with tears he cannot hide.

God has blessed you richly,
May He continue to bless you in every way.
In turn, give Him praises,
For your love, your lives, and your wedding day!

Written July 9, 2011

*"He is the one you praise; he is your God, who performed for you
those great and awesome wonders you saw with your own eyes."*
Deuteronomy 10:21

Monumental Moments

Your baby is here,
Nestled in your arms.
A touch of heaven,
A joy beyond compare.

Then there are times,
He is crying and crying.
You are tired and weary,
You feel discouraged.

The highs are higher,
The lows are lower
Than you ever imagined.
Words can't really describe
The job you've been given.

Take each moment
To breathe and take in
The time you have
To love this child.

God will give you
The strength you need.
He will carry you through it
And give you and your baby
   Blessed sleep,
   Wonderful smiles,
   Monumental moments,
Time with your child!

Written May 11, 2009

"He gives strength to the weary
and increases the power of the weak."
Isaiah 40:29

More Beautiful Than Before

A vision of faith and newfound strength,
You carry your scars so well.
God has chosen you for this very purpose,
You have an amazing story to tell.

Healing throughout your body,
Redemption for your soul.
Just like Jesus carries our burdens,
You have been given this special role.

You have beauty from within,
That we all truly adore
And these words are meant for you,
You are more beautiful than before.

So many people carry scars from illnesses, and sometimes the scars are deep within. Perhaps you are one of those people. Remember, you are more beautiful (or handsome) than before!

"She is clothed with strength and dignity;
she can laugh at the days to come."
Proverbs 31:25

Morning of Prayer

I stood in the chapel,
A morning dark and cold.
Music filled the air,
Laughter all around,
Candles everywhere.

Then it was time for prayer,
You filled us with Your presence,
And anointed us with oil.
The Holy Spirit breathing
And our spirits oh so still.

The quiet was only broken,
By tears or whispered prayer.
The scene was magnificent,
A present from our Lord.

Prayer can change us,
It can change other's lives.
We can connect uniquely,
Through the miracle of prayer.

Written January 5, 2010

Our women's Bible study group met one cold January morning for a quiet morning of prayer in the sanctuary. What a morning it was. Time for reflection. Time to listen to beautiful music. Someone taking time to listen to my prayer requests with her heart, anointing me with oil, and praying with me. What a life-changing experience!

"In the morning, Lord, you hear my voice;
in the morning I lay my requests before you
and wait expectantly."
Psalm 5:3

Mother's Day

She walks with style and grace,
An ageless sense of beauty.
Time may have slowed her pace
But her love of others is unfailing.

She talks and talks and talks some more,
Her family and friends she holds dear.
She's the mother we adore,
She's the one, the only Mom!

Happy Mother's Day!

Written for my mom on May 13, 2006

"Therefore, we do not lose heart. Though outwardly we are
wasting away, yet inwardly we are being renewed day by day."
2 Corinthians 4:16

My Beloved

I miss your smile,
Your eyes caressing mine.
I miss your hugs,
Your strong arms that hold me tight.
I miss our talks,
Our words conveyed with love.
I miss your voice,
The strong and happy bass.
I miss your touch,
Your gentle hand on mine.
I know I can make it,
You will be back in a day!

Written November 3, 1987

My husband had been out of town for three weeks, and that was the longest we had been apart. For some reason that was hard on me, even though he worked out of town a lot. I still remember teaching during the day, and being as happy as I could be. Then I would walk in the house, and sadness took over me.

"Trust in him at all times, you people;
pour out your hearts to him,
for God is our refuge."
Psalm 62:8

My Friend

She whirls into your life
And it's somehow better.
Because her spirit is glowing
And her heart is always showing.

She cares for her, she cares for him,
She cares for me and lets me know it.
She sometimes wanders here and there
All the while, trying to be fair.

A friend for years she has been,
My sister in a special way.
Someone who knows me so well,
Friends for life, you can tell.

Today is a gift of life,
We cherish it so much.
We remember fondly the past,
Our future as friends will last!

Sometimes we have a friend who is so full of life. And we are so fortunate if that person is a friend for life!

"Praise be to the God and Father of our Lord Jesus Christ! In his great mercy he has given us new birth into a living hope through the resurrection of Jesus Christ from the dead, and into an inheritance that can never perish, spoil or fade. This inheritance is kept in heaven for you."
1 Peter 1:3-4

My Grandson and Me

Driving to and from daycare,
With my grandson in his car seat,
I had an idea,
I thought was pretty neat.

Instead of pointing out,
White cars and trucks that were red,
I changed it up a bit
This is what I said:

"Do you want me to sing
Jesus Loves Me?" And then—
I looked in the rearview mirror,
He nodded his head—to me meant Amen!

We sang that song over and over,
I knew he liked it
By the smile on his face.
It felt like a grandma and grandson hit.

The best part was when I saw this happen,
He took out his binkie and sang along.
Those awesome moments started simply,
By me asking—Do you want me to sing a song?

Written November 1, 2009

This poem goes to the heart of grandparents, parents, sisters, brothers, friends everywhere. One of the greatest opportunities we have is to share Jesus with a little child. I will never forget that moment in the van singing "Jesus Loves Me" with my grandson.

Who knows, maybe there is a child in your life who is waiting for you to do the same!

"But from everlasting to everlasting
the Lord's love is with those who fear him,
and his righteousness with their children's children—"
Psalm 103:17

My Guy

So much energy
To fill each day,
Full of purpose,
Do it fast!

Sweet and gentle,
Bold and quick,
I love all of you,
You're an amazing man!

Written May 1, 2012

Written to my husband on my five-year cancer-free anniversary. We were going out to celebrate!

"The Lord has done it this very day;
let us rejoice today and be glad."
Psalm 118:24

My Gypsy Friend

She loves adventure,
For what lies ahead,
The mountains are calling,
She is on her way!

One day Colorado,
Another south of France,
Or maybe she'll explore,
All the mountain tops!

Some have said
She has a gypsy spirit,
That's so true,
My gypsy friend!

Written on May 1, 2012

Written to a friend before she headed to Colorado in the RV. Adventure, fun, and living life to the fullest!

"You make known to me the path of life; you will fill me with joy in your presence, with eternal pleasures at your right hand."
Psalm 16:11

My Hairdresser Extraordinaire!

She smiles and listens to my stories,
Grandbabies, families, jobs, wedding days,
It's a list never-ending.
She even sounds interested in so many ways!

Sure, sometimes she's changed my color to pink,
Or gives me a Mohawk buzz.
We laugh and drink a glass of bubbly,
You know why? It's because. . .

She's amazing! She's wonderful!
She's my hairdresser extraordinaire!
She loves me, and you know what?
She loves my hair!

Written December 22, 2008

It is amazing how you become close to someone you see a lot over the years. I was just kidding about the pink hair, the mohawk buzz, and the glass of bubbly. We didn't need those things to laugh a lot!

"Indeed, the very hairs of your head are all numbered.
Don't be afraid; you are worth more than many sparrows."
Luke 12:7

My Love, My Friend

God told me this morning to get on my knees
And pray for you like never before.
To thank Him for all He has made you to be,
To cherish the love of husband and wife.

He told me you need this every day,
What surprised me is what He whispered next,
"This devotion to prayer is the only way
To keep your love going and keep bitterness at bay!"

So, I opened my Bible to His Word,
He showed me Song of Songs.
"Tell him how much he's loved," this is what I heard
And tears sprang to my eyes.

My love, my friend, my protector, and more.
Your smile, your heart, your touch, your kiss.
Your soul, your spirit—It's you I adore.
I'm so thankful God brought us together.

Looking to the future as well as the past,
We may be in our autumn years,
Our love is strong and meant to last,
Of this I am certain!

Written December 31, 2008

"I belong to my beloved,
and his desire is for me."
Song of Songs 7:10

My Prayer

Lord I bow humbly before your throne,
Help me take each thought captive
And make it as your own.
To love my neighbor as myself,
To discover your wisdom and your true wealth.
Rich in blessings, that is so true,
The air I breathe, family, life,
The Bible to name a few.
May I pray night and day
And ponder your words in my heart.
Thank you, Jesus, for being The Way!

Written November 28, 2008

"Lord, hear my prayer,
listen to my cry for mercy;
in your faithfulness and righteousness
come to my relief."
Psalm 143:1

My Tribute to You

I asked of you a little time,
You gave your heart instead.
My little girl I gladly shared,
For I know that you are led

The love of Jesus is in your eyes.
I can hear Him in your laugh,
Your sense of humor is unsurpassed,
I know He guides your path!

Farewell is too hard to say,
Instead I'll say, "Bye for now."
Just think, before Him in heaven,
Together we'll praise and bow!

Written May 20, 1987

I wrote this for a wonderful Christian woman who ran a daycare. She loved each child in such a special way. They prayed before every snack and meal. The children saw Jesus through the actions and love of this woman!

"And do not forget to do good and to share with others,
for with such sacrifices God is pleased."
Hebrews 13:16

Never

Have you had times
Filled with people
Yet you felt alone?
At times, that's me.

This morning I took a walk,
Those waves of loneliness
Washed over me
Took me by surprise.

As I walked this beautiful morning,
Birds were singing,
People walking on the trail,
The sky, sun, flowers.

My heart started to fill.
All those signs,
I felt comfort,
No longer alone!

Written July 17, 2014

Written after a walk on a beautiful summer day. I was alone. Or was I?

"Be strong and courageous. Do not be afraid or terrified because
of them, for the Lord your God goes with you; he will never leave
you nor forsake you."
Deuteronomy 31:6

Oasis

Your home is an oasis,
A place for rest and restoration.
Welcoming friends with laughter and fun,
Wonderful music in the air,
A glass of wine and meals sublime.

She has energy unending,
Enthusiastic about every detail.
Running her hands on the keyboard,
Singing with a love-filled heart.
Touching people far and near,
Missions with so many interests.

He has unending stories to share,
Laughing, working, playing, giving,
A pillar of strength.
Watching moving flowers or building a business,
Enjoying life to the max,
So many reasons to celebrate.

Your home truly is an oasis!

Written April 13, 2009

Have you been in someone's home and it feels like an oasis? You should tell them! It' a little slice of heaven!

"Sarah said, 'God has brought me laughter, and everyone who hears about this will laugh with me.'"
Genesis 21:6

On My Knees

I'm on my knees
Praising God for a birthday
Beyond my dreams.
One more soul in heaven
To live for You.
On earth and for eternity,
Bless this person Father,
Hold him in your hand,
Fill him with your Spirit,
Faith, peace, comfort,
Strength, hope, and love,
Thank you, Jesus!

Written June 22, 2010

"We praise you, God,
we praise you, for your Name is near;
people tell of your wonderful deeds."
Psalm 75:1

Once in a Lifetime

I never could have guessed so many years ago
Our friendship would bloom and grow.
Times were simple, and we had some fun,
Fries at the bookstore, listening to "Da Do Run Run."

We jaywalked, you cheered, we sang the school fight song,
"Go Bluejays, spell SPIRIT," the list goes on and on.
How many nights did we laugh and talk?
Our friendship was cemented and solid as a rock!

Before we knew it, graduation time was near,
Good-bye to high school, face the future with no fear.
Best friends in high school, why not college too?
New friends, Debbie and Rita, just to name a few.

Our friendship moved to adulthood, with husbands, children
and homes.
The years did not escape us. We had coffee and phones!
Sharing joys and pains and dreams of tomorrow,
Funny, crazy, silly antics and moments of sorrow.

You have been a special friend in so many ways,
I cherish our past together and look forward to future days!
Happy 50th birthday wishes I send,
To my once in a lifetime friend!

Written February 14, 1999

Isn't it amazing when you have a friend you have known for years? That is such a special bond and such a wonderful blessing!

"A friend loves at all times,
and a brother is born for a time of adversity."
Proverbs 17:17

Only God Would Know

So long ago our paths would cross
And now you are by my side.
Working, giving, growing, learning,
My heart is filled with pride!

I look into your face and see an angel,
Sent to this time and place.
Running the race with me,
Our lives filled with honor and grace!

The Saints cheer us onward,
The Lamb, the Comforter, the Spirit call us by name
To have faith that moves mountains
Practicing forgiveness and not laying blame!

Only God would know
What a blessing you are to me!

Written April 24, 2002

This poem could apply to so many people in my life, and I am so thankful!

> *"I thank my God every time I remember you.*
> *In all my prayers for all of you, I always pray with joy."*
> *Philippians 1:3-4*

Open My Eyes

Lord, open my eyes so I can see:
 Your presence everywhere,
 Your light in my life,
 Your love shining on me,
 Your hope burning bright!

Lord, open my eyes so I can see:
 Your face to focus on,
 Your strength from within,
 Your friendship in my soul.

Sometimes I take my eyes off You,
 I allow others to take away my joy.
 I let them chip away at who I am.
 I don't focus on your life-giving light.

Lord, open my eyes so I can see:
 My heavenly life,
 My heavenly home.
 My heavenly blessings,
 Your heavenly presence,

All because of You!

Written on July 18, 2013

This could be our love letter to Jesus!

"Though you have not seen him, you love him; and even though you do not see him now, you believe in him and are filled with an inexpressible and glorious joy, for you are receiving the end result of your faith, the salvation of your souls."
1 Peter 1:8-9

Our Guard

He greets us with a smile each day,
A friend to one and all.
Eager to share a news story,
Or the weather—winter, spring, summer, and fall!

He seems to know just what to say
And gives a smile or a listening ear.
Ready to have a great big laugh,
Or sympathize with a tear!

He guards much more than our safety,
Growing his faith—It's the Bible he reads
And when the timing is perfect,
He shares his faith to fill other's needs!

Written March 23, 2007

This poem was written for our security guard at work. Over the years, I had watched how people were drawn to him. He was there for everyone, and he really cared. One day, I kept thinking of what a blessing he was to so many people, and these words came to me. I wrote them down, and then I kept them. I didn't tell him because I thought he would think I was crazy to write a poem about him. Then one morning I walked into work, and there was our guard. I knew I needed to tell him about the poem. His response to me was, "You wrote a poem about me? I want to see it!" I quickly typed the poem and printed a copy for him. Then I stood quietly while he read it. When he finished he had a big smile and told me he was going to frame that poem. Then he asked me to sign it. I talked to him later, and he told me he made lots of copies of the poem and gave them to people. It sounded like he told lots of people about that poem. Often

I would greet him at his desk and he would thank me for that poem. It was neat to see how touched he was.

"But grow in the grace and knowledge of our Lord and Savior Jesus Christ. To him be glory both now and forever! Amen."
2 Peter 3:18

Over Pastry and Coffee

Over pastry and coffee
We grow closer to Him.
We share
  Laughter, tears,
  Hopes, fears,
God brought us together
So many years ago.
This we know for certain,
We love Him so!

Holy Spirit fill us
As we walk upon the earth.
May we keep our zeal
And wonder of new birth.

Alive in Jesus
Is our bold prayer.
For all those around us,
Humbly we serve and share.

Thank you for your friendship,
Our spirits soar to the brim.
Over pastry and coffee,
We grow closer to Him!

Written January 15, 2010

Do you have a friend that you meet for coffee and talk about Jesus? The coffee and pastry are great. Talking about our faith in Jesus puts those moments over the top!

"Therefore, as God's chosen people, holy and dearly loved, clothe yourselves with compassion, kindness, humility, gentleness and patience."
Colossians 3:12

Precious Friend

Time to laugh, time to share,
Time to be together.
Often our souls to bare,
A true friend is silver.

This friendship is part of God's plan,
Knowing His timing is perfect.
Brought together as only God can,
A true friend is gold.

Words from each other blending,
Unspoken ones understood.
Joy we know God is sending,
A true friend is a rose.

Sometimes silver, sometimes gold,
Sometimes a rose to enjoy,
Sometimes timid, sometimes bold,
A true friend forever!

Written February 2, 1990

I realized how rich we are when we have a precious friend!

"My command is this: Love each other as I have loved you.
Greater love has no one than this:
to lay down one's life for one's friends."
John 15:12-13

Retirement

I know retirement is a near and distant land,
I don't know what's in store for us
But I know Who holds our hand!

Riches we are given in life,
Children, spouses, and music in the air,
The love between husband and wife!

God has so much to give,
He is there with outstretched hands
For us to really live!

All we have to do is trust in Him
To provide the miracles of the day,
He knows where we're going and where we've been!

Written March 26, 2007

I read this at my retirement party. I had no clue what retirement would mean for me. That is the beauty of a new adventure!

*"Trust in the Lord with all your heart
and lean not on your own understanding;
in all your ways submit to him,
and he will make your paths straight."
Proverbs 3:5-6*

Sealed With A Kiss

Who is that handsome Navy man
Smiling at the love of his life?
That sexy woman with auburn hair,
Was soon to be his wife
And so, fifty years ago, their love was sealed with a kiss.

Those romantic years flew by so fast,
Then along came daughter number one.
Dirty diapers and bottles and rattles and toys,
They repeated to each other—This is fun!
And when there was time, their love was sealed with a kiss.

Along came another daughter—you know what that means
Dolls and babies and dresses galore.
Putting toys together on Christmas Eve
And then getting up at 4:00
And if they remembered, their love was sealed with a kiss.

And then came the surprise of their life,
At their age, they were having a third.
"It's a boy! It's a boy!"
They spread the word until everyone had heard,
Then they smiled and laughed, the moment was sealed with a kiss.

A family of five was a busy life
Swimming, picnics, and vacations.
Remember that line in Colorado
"Look at those mountains! It's no time for relaxation!"
That time was silver, and it was sealed with a kiss.

One by one the children left
And had families of their own,
But mom and dad didn't twiddle their thumbs,

As helpers, travelers, and dancers they were known.
Retirement was pretty nice! Happy times were sealed with a kiss.

Here you are today—that handsome Navy man,
That sexy woman with auburn hair.
After fifty years together
You still make a handsome pair.
June 20, 1993—A Golden Time
Your marriage is sealed with a kiss!

I wrote this for our parent's fiftieth anniversary, and I read it at their party. They loved it! My dad made a copy and put it in a plastic protector. I am pretty sure that for quite a while they showed it to every person who visited them. One of the gifts we gave them was A Precious Moment figurine of a couple and the phrase Sealed With A Kiss. It was a great celebration!

"We love because he first loved us."
1 John 4:19

Sixteen Years

Happy Anniversary, to my husband of sixteen years.
There have been so many good times,
There also have been tears,
It takes both to keep us close.

Those first years were so precious.
An apartment and two bikes,
The kitchen wasn't spacious
But a couple we were there!

Next came the thrill of our first home.
It even had a pool!
For two, we had three phones!
The memories there are many!

We know that God has blessed us
With a son and two daughters.
They smiled and laughed and sometimes fussed
But we are raising them together!

After sixteen years I love you more than ever
And I'm proud to be your wife.
I hope it lasts forever!
Happy Anniversary, to my husband of sixteen years!

Written May 20, 1987 for our sixteenth wedding anniversary.

"Many waters cannot quench love;
rivers cannot sweep it away.
If one were to give
all the wealth of one's house for love,
it would be utterly scorned."
Song of Songs 8:7

Someday in Heaven

Someday in heaven
As believers we will be,
Praising Lord Jesus
And laughing with glee!

While we are here
Let's open our eyes,
Let's treasure the moments
Time really flies!

Someday in heaven
We'll recount every time
We laughed, we cried,
Believers sublime!

Someday in heaven
As believers we will be,
Filled with the Spirit
And laughing with glee!

Written January 18, 2012

*"But our citizenship is in heaven. And we eagerly await a Savior
from there, the Lord Jesus Christ, who, by the power that enables
him to bring everything under his control, will transform our lowly
bodies so that they will be like his glorious body."*
Philippians 3:20-21

Someone is 90!

Who in the world is 90 today?
Who has lived almost a century?
Who has traveled through the ages with style?
Who greets everyone with a laugh and a smile?

The answer is resounding in the air,
Dad, dad, dad is the cheer!
You are honored here today,
We love you is what we say!

10, 20, 30, 40, 50, 60, 70, 80, 90
Those sure are a large number of years.
You can't be that old—there's not a chance,
You're still working in the garden and taking mom to a dance!

Happy Birthday to you—the man of the hour.
We really enjoy celebrating with you today,
We appreciate your soul and heart,
You're kind, still young, and really smart!

Happy 90th Birthday!!!!!!!!!!

Written June 7, 2008

This poem was written for my dad for his ninetieth birthday. The immediate family went to my mom and dad's favorite Italian restaurant to help him celebrate. There were about twenty of us including two in high chairs. There was a lot of commotion, lots of talking and laughing, and lots of food. He loved it!

"Every good and perfect gift is from above, coming down from the Father of the heavenly lights, who does not change like shifting shadows. He chose to give us birth through the word of truth, that we might be a kind of first fruits of all he created."
James 1:17-18

Sometimes

Sometimes I think that I'm so strong,
In my spirit and my mind
I can handle anything,
A crisis of any kind.

Then something comes along
And tears begin to fall.
My strength starts to fade,
My spirit is not strong at all.

It's okay to say we're weak,
We need the prayers of others.
It's times like that
We really need our sisters and our brothers!

Isn't it shocking when one thing changes in our world, and we find we are not as strong as we thought? Sometimes, it is just the thought of something happening, something that shakes our world. And sometimes, it is just the little things that tip the scale, and the tears begin to fall. It's okay. God wants us to lift up one another and to let Him carry us through!

This poem was written two days after we had a big family celebration for my mom's ninetieth birthday. The party was wonderful with lots of food and fun. We sang happy birthday to my mom and then to my one-year-old grandson, who clapped his hands in glee. The day was wonderful. Then on Tuesday, which just happened to be election day, I called my mom. Her voice sounded different. Strained and weak. She had fallen, and I suddenly saw how fragile her life was. I was shocked at my reaction. I couldn't stop crying, just thinking of the idea of losing her. The good news is that even though she was a little banged up, she was going strong.

"Come to me, all you who are weary and burdened, and I will give you rest. Take my yoke upon you and learn from me, for I am gentle and humble in heart, and you will find rest for your souls."
Matthew 11:28-29

Sometimes I Feel Invisible

Sometimes I feel invisible,
Sometimes all alone.
I shouldn't say it, but
Sometimes I feel dumb.
I try to push through it
And smile along the way.
No one will know
If I am hurting today.
The number <u>one</u> keeps
Popping in my head.
One verse, one song
One call to a friend
Reminds me of
The One and only One
Who makes me
Not invisible.
Makes me whole,
This is God's Son!

Written October 1, 2008

"For in him all things were created: things in heaven and on earth, visible and invisible, whether thrones or powers or rulers or authorities; all things have been created through him and for him."
Colossians 1:16

Take the Step

No, Lord, that isn't what I had in mind!
I really don't want to go there.
Sure, there's a blessing waiting for me
But I may get hurt along the way.

And then the Spirit urges me,
I feel my strength increase.
To get where God is leading,
I have to take the step.

The first step is the hardest,
To commit to that path.
He gently walks beside me
And smiles as I am blessed!

Written April 24, 2008

"Direct my footsteps according to your word;
let no sin rule over me."
Psalm 119:133

Take Time

I appreciate the moment,
I appreciate the day,
Because all of you are in it,
What more can I say?

Yesterday is over,
Tomorrow isn't here.
Today is a present,
For laughs or even a tear.

Take time to really listen,
Take time to really care,
So just one person
Won't say, "Life is not fair!"

Written July 12, 2005

When I led a training team at a corporation, I left a morning message on their phones every day. Usually I woke up early and left the message. Sometimes I even woke up in the middle of the night. Sometimes they were silly like the time I was excited about our upcoming outing to a baseball game. I left an enthusiastic message and pretended that I had something to sing. Then I put my husband on the phone, and he sang Take Me Out To The Ballgame in his low baritone voice. It was hilarious! Later some of the trainers told me they kept that message for a long time because it made them laugh.

It took courage for me to write this poem for my training team and to read it for the morning message. I'm glad I did!

"The Lord has done it this very day;
let us rejoice today and be glad."
Psalm 118:24

Tears of Joy

Sometimes you're allowed to step back
To see what is dear in your life.
A husband who partners your soul,
Daughters like gems, and a son with a wonderful wife,
Friends close as family and God by your side.

Tears of joy may stream down your cheeks,
Let them flow because they do what words cannot say.
A part of yourself you freely give,
You know God has given you this day,
A present like no others.

Laughter and giggles and jokes abound,
A drink in hand to start this special date.
It's blue as the ocean and smooth as silk,
What more could I want I ask this of you?

A BIG BOX OF CHOCOLATES AND TIRAMISU!!!!!!!!!

Written June 19, 2004

> *"They will come with weeping;*
> *they will pray as I bring them back.*
> *I will lead them beside streams of water*
> *on a level path where they will not stumble,*
> *because I am Israel's father,*
> *and Ephraim is my firstborn son."*
> *Jeremiah 31:9*

Thank You

Thank you for your smile so ready,
For your touch when I am blue,
For the words of loving admiration,
It feels good to be close to you!

Countless miles hand in hand,
Through sun, wind and rain,
May we draw closer and closer,
Our love won't stay the same.

Thank you for the tears so freely
That have fallen on your cheek,
Laughing and crying we have shared as one
Sometimes with no need to speak.

These words of love I give you,
I know that I must say,
Our love is greater than before,
Tomorrow more than today!

I wrote this poem in the 1970s. Even back then we took long walks
hand in hand. Today we are still known as that couple that takes long
walks hand in hand. I remember a little plaque that said in French
"Je t'aime plus qu'hier moins que damain." I love you more than
yesterday, less than tomorrow.

"Be devoted to one another in love.
Honor one another above yourselves."
Romans 12:10

Thank You Mom

The presents are wrapped, the tree is lit
And the desserts make a beautiful display.
Making memories year after year,
How do you do it—we all say!

When we were young, you never slept
And you sewed on Christmas Eve.
Now that we're grown it's so much fun,
Chaos and noise until we leave!

So, thanks for everything,
We appreciate it—we really do.
Characteristics like yours are hard to find,
Laughing, giving—just to name a few!

Merry Christmas!

I wrote this for my mom. As an adult I had a new appreciation for
the way my mom made Christmas so special for us!

> *"He will yet fill your mouth with laughter*
> *and your lips with shouts of joy."*
> *Job 8:21*

That Special Couple

Both had hair of gray and smiles upon each face.
A lovely blue carnation upon the dress she wore,
Without words, their eyes said to each other,
"It's you I adore!"

He held her arm tenderly
And caressed her with his smile.
She returned the adoring look,
Just engaged a little while!

May your love be renewed
And be like that loving pair.
God has given you to each other
Your whole lives to share!

Written May 10, 1990

I happened to meet an older couple, and we started to chat. They told me they were recently engaged. They were adorably in love!

"Love is patient, love is kind.
It does not envy, it does not boast, it is not proud."
1 Corinthians 13:4

The Caregiver

He kneels on bended knee
To caress his lady's feet.
A humble act of love
For his wife of many years.

Together they make one,
Finishing sentences,
Asking questions over and over,
Making it through each day.

Taking time to laugh,
Looking back on younger times,
Forward to time with family and friends,
A long life they've been given.

Some days are extra hard,
Pain and illness take their toll,
Others holding them in prayer,
Asking for healing and relief.

It is amazing when you think
How many things these two have done,
How many places they have been,
How many lives they have touched.

May today they find some joy,
Today they find relief.
May the sun shine extra bright
And God cover them with His love.

Written for my parents when they were age ninety-two and nine-ty-one. Mom had multiple health issues, and dad patiently and lovingly took care of her.

"Husbands, love your wives, just as Christ loved the church
and gave himself up for her."
Ephesians 5:25

The Challenge

You came to me for help
And gladly I said yes,
But I have one hesitation
And this fear I must confess.

Together we can make your light so bright
With our minds side by side,
But what if you turn away
And run from me and hide.

Will the light that was once so strong,
With its beam reaching to the sky,
Slowly begin to fade and dim
And one day even die.

This fear I hope will never be
And instead just the opposite is true.
Your light grows brighter every day
And together each challenge we will pursue!

Written May 1990

I tutored high school students for a while. It was frustrating when I saw so much potential, and the student wouldn't try. I am an enthusiastic teacher, so I would do my best to help the student be enthusiastic about learning.

"Carry each other's burdens, and in this way,
you will fulfill the law of Christ."
Galatians 6:2

The College Graduate

You're a graduate,
That is absolutely great.
Your hard work was worth it,
Those hours of studying late!

Bring on the caffeine,
Turn off the fun.
You have papers to write
And perfect they must be done!

A degree with honors,
We're so proud of you.
You're an amazing person
And a college graduate too!

Written May 15, 2004

A friend went to college after she was in the work world for many years. It takes a lot of dedication, hard work, encouragement from others and caffeine!

"'For I know the plans I have for you,' declares the Lord,
'plans to prosper you and not to harm you,
plans to give you hope and a future.'"
Jeremiah 29:11

The Cross of Christ

You see others through Jesus's eyes.
The cross is right before you,
Surrounded by a crowd
Or quiet times of prayer.

Continue on your exciting journey,
Daily feeding on the Word.
Then in the world so uniquely,
The cross of Christ shines in you!

Written January 6, 2010

This poem applies to anyone who lets his or her faith shine. Those people have Jesus eyes!

"Ears that hear and eyes that see—
the Lord has made them both."
Proverbs 20:12

The Faith of a Child

With a smile on his face
He greets everyone he meets.
Not a worry in his head,
Everything is new and exciting!

If only we would do the same,
Experience the newness of life.
Live in the moment
And run to our Father with open arms!

The faith of a child!

June 21, 2011

This morning in my Bible study, one of the gals talked about her two-year-old grandson. He loved meeting new people and even shook their hand. He ran with open arms to the people he loved. Such enthusiasm. The illustration of running with outstretched arms was the perfect illustration of "The Faith of a Child!"

"Jesus said, 'Let the little children come to me, and do not hinder them, for the kingdom of heaven belongs to such as these.'"
Matthew 19:14

The Future

It's more than I can bear.
You have a plan for me?
I just have to take Your hand?
Then help me hold on tight.
Carry me through this, carry me through.

Someday my strength is waning
And it's hard to walk ahead,
But daily you have shown me
That we're not two, but <u>One</u> instead.
Thank you, God for carrying me through this,
For carrying me through.

Written May 15, 1987

"May the God of hope fill you with all joy and
peace as you trust in him, so that you may overflow
with hope by the power of the Holy Spirit."
Romans 15:13

The Grandfather Clock Without A Heart

We walked into the house
And everything was bare,
Except for the grandfather clock
Standing over there.

So many memories.
Grandma & grandpa, mom & dad,
Seeing the house empty
Makes us a little sad.

All those years;
Laughter, activities, lots of food,
Babies, toddlers, teenagers too,
These thoughts lift our mood.

How many times
Did we walk in the door
And not really notice
That clock on the floor?

Then it was time
To say good-bye.
The house, the home,
We said with a sigh.

Several of us
Around the clock we stood,
Taking in the sight,
Touching the wood.

Gently opening the door
Where the pendulum should be,
We were all astonished
At what we did see.

Empty and without a heart,
It had remained all those years,
It was just a box.
There was laughter! Absolutely no tears!

Sometimes we think
A treasure is there.
Sometimes we don't realize
The treasure is bare!

Written October 16, 2013

Dad passed away almost two years ago, and mom moved to an assisted living. It took a long time to empty the house, and it was finally time to put it on the market. There was only one thing left, the grandfather clock. Mom never talked about it much. It seemed to just be sitting there in the living room. A friend was storing the clock at mom and dad's, so we thought someone would take it one day.

Then we made the decision to move the clock out of the house. We assumed it was a treasure that we just hadn't noticed before. Imagine our surprise when we opened the door and saw it was just a box made to look like a grandfather clock. It made us laugh. We had taken so many steps to move that treasure, and then we realized it wasn't a treasure at all.

Somehow that seemed fitting to leave the house while laughing. There had been a lot of laughter in that home all those years.

"Do not store up for yourselves treasures on earth, where moths and vermin destroy, and where thieves break in and steal. But store up for yourselves treasures in heaven, where moths and vermin do not destroy, and where thieves do not break in and steal."
Matthew 6:19-20

The One

He was just a baby in my arms
And the focus of my life.
I prayed that in God's timing,
He would find a wonderful wife.

My prayers were answered!
I have met her face to face.
She's the one I knew was out there,
In my heart, she will have a special place.

As they walk life's path together
In rough times and times of fun,
May they be reminded God united them,
May they hold each other and whisper,
"You're the one!"

Written August 20, 2003. This was written for our son and his new fiancé. Such exciting times!

"Be completely humble and gentle;
be patient, bearing with one another in love."
Ephesians 4:2

The Pain

I know the pain is real,
It's in my heart and soul.
The tugging is there, and my shell is cracking.
The tears, the yearning—Lord, what shall I do?
Do I wait until the timing is just right?
Or keep knocking on doors to find my place?
One minute I'm sure and confidence is mine,
The next I'm wondering what to do with my time.
Lord, take away this emptiness inside.
Fill me with purpose, with Your goal ahead.
Help me count for eternity!

Written September 22, 1987

I was a stay at home mom for lots of years, and I have so many wonderful memories. Then I had a yearning to use my brain in another way and contribute out in the world. It's okay to acknowledge when we are going through hard times. That makes the good times that much better!

> *"From the ends of the earth I call to you,*
> *I call as my heart grows faint;*
> *lead me to the rock that is higher than I."*
> *Psalm 61:2*

The Pattern of Life

We are all vulnerable in some sort of way.
Am I living well? Are my motives right?
Am I listening to God throughout the day?
Am I fulfilling the purpose He gives to me?

Look at Jesus and see the pattern of life
Doing good, receiving praise, and yet,
Spirit-led on His path, in spite of strife,
His heart always focusing on the Father.

We learn from each other,
We learn from the Word of God,
In Him we grow as sisters and brothers,
Each child, each woman, each man!

Every day, there is so much to explore,
It's the pattern of life,
To bring God glory!

Written April 16, 2008

"A generous person will prosper;
whoever refreshes others will be refreshed."
Proverbs 11:24

The Power of Prayer

Oh Lord,
Help us on our journey with You;
Filled with your Spirit,
To see the power of prayer,
To believe the power of prayer,
To be vessels for the power of prayer,
To wait expectantly,
To live expectantly,
To praise expectantly,
To go through trials expectantly,
To serve expectantly,
To love expectantly,
To pray expectantly,
And yes, to die expectantly.
Expecting your power,
Expecting your grace,
Expecting your love,
Expecting your forgiveness,
Expecting your majesty,
Expecting your peace.

Thank you, Holy Spirit,
For others you lay on our hearts.
Help us to pray boldly
Even when it appears hopeless.
Help us remember
You have the power
To breathe life
Into dry bones.

Thank you, Father
For the way you work in our lives.
You know our hurts,
You know our pains,

You know our victories,
You hear our prayers and praises.
Thank you for the power of prayer
And the way you use us.
We humbly lay our requests
At the feet of Jesus
And wait expectantly!
Thank you, for answered prayer!
Amen!

Written January 13, 2010

This poem came to me after a Bible study on praying boldly for our loves ones who don't know Jesus. "Pray boldly in the Spirit's power as if you would be shocked if He didn't answer it."

"Is anyone among you in trouble? Let them pray.
Is anyone happy? Let them sing songs of praise."
James 5:13

The Red Convertible

We are driving down the road of life,
The wind in our hair and a smile on our face.
The red convertible bonding husband and wife,
So much fun and such a blessing!

I look at my car and this is what I see:
Love from you beyond compare,
You took all that time to pick it out for me!
It touches my heart over and over!

My favorite times are you by my side.
It doesn't matter who's behind the wheel,
Sweet words, "Let's take a drive!"
I love my car, and I cherish you with me!

The red convertible is really mine,
I tell myself repeatedly.
I love to share the story and have my face shine.
You surprised me with the gift of a lifetime!

Written March 25, 2008

I was totally shocked when a red convertible was waiting for me in our garage! It wasn't my birthday or any special event. My husband is frugal so I would never have guessed that he would do this. Over the years I have had so much fun in this red convertible, and I have had so much fun sharing it with others!

"For where your treasure is, there your heart will be also."
Matthew 6:21

This Day Forward

How were we to know,
Eleven years after the day
He slipped the ring on my finger,
That you would come our way?

A squinting little bundle,
Giving no indication of your energy
And vibrant look at life.
Our family was complete with you three.

From little on you've been there,
A buddy by my side.
So many great accomplishments,
Today I'm filled with pride!

To know the Lord and love Him
And walk your life with Him
Will be your greatest victory,
The choices are within.

The future is uncertain
And it's hard to make a plan.
Keep using that talent
We will be your biggest fan!

Written May 19, 1996

This is a poem I wrote for the confirmation day at church for one of our children. It was a time to acknowledge their faith journey. We are all growing. That is why it is called a journey!

"Create in me a pure heart, O God,
and renew a steadfast spirit within me."
Psalm 51:10

This Journey

I recognize this path,
Yet it comes as a surprise,
What once was vague,
Is now clearly in my mind.

You're telling me to totally trust
And You will lead the way.
"Take My hand, I'm here
Before you, beside you, and behind
It is all part of My design."

And so, I walk
Where I've been before,
Sometimes afraid and sometimes not,
Of what the future holds.

Written on June 27, 2018

"Let the morning bring me word of your unfailing love,
for I have put my trust in you.
Show me the way I should go,
for to you I entrust my life."
Psalm 143:8

Time

Time, time, it passes so quickly.
One minute I'm a bride, the next I'll be forty,
More gray hairs, oh Lordy!

Looking back, what do I remember most?
Long walks with Les,
Naps hand in hand with our youngest,
I've long forgotten when my house was a mess!

There were moments at the piano with our second,
And reading books with her,
And lots of laughs with our son.
Oh, don't let the years be a blur!

Lord, help me savor these moments
And truly be the queen of my home.
Loving my king, prince and princesses
And knowing that I'm not alone!

Written May 29, 1987

> *"You have made my days a mere handbreadth;*
> *the span of my years is as nothing before you.*
> *Everyone is but a breath,*
> *even those who seem secure."*
> *Psalm 39:5*

Time to Go

I can picture it now,
There's happiness in your soul
And a smile on your face.
I clearly know my role.
While you meet and greet,
Organize, arrange and unpack,
I quietly observe
And admit the fact
That soon I will hear these words,
"It's time to go."
My eyes will cloud,
Because I love you so.
It's hard to explain,
When the last leaves the nest.
My brain says it's okay
But my heart knows the rest!

Written August 16, 2000

Having a child go away to college is often a great growing experience for the child and for the parents. Letting go can be bittersweet.

*"Start children off on the way they should go,
and even when they are old they will not turn from it."*
Proverbs 22:6

To Be Chosen

What do you say when you
See the hand of God?
To be chosen from so many
Is beyond my wildest dreams.
How do they know what longings
Are in my heart?
What gives me comfort and peace
Is having God on my side.
To trust in things unseen,
To trust Him to do what is best,
To trust Him in everything!

Written October 12, 1992

I was chosen from hundreds of applicants to interview for a job I was very interested in. I couldn't get over how they chose me! I didn't get the job. God had someplace else in mind for me!

"Humble yourselves, therefore, under God's mighty hand,
that he may lift you up in due time."
1 Peter 5:6

To Have And To Hold

To have and to hold from this day forward.
Our words from so long ago.
Who would guess that after 36 years
We would love each other so!

I am here for you
And you are here for me.
Entwined with a kiss or touch,
Love from God as it should be!

I recommit my heart this day,
To my husband, lover, and friend,
Let's live our vows forever,
As two souls to one we blend!

Written on January 8, 2008

*"That is why a man leaves his father and mother and
is united to his wife, and they become one flesh."*
Genesis 2:24

To Mom

Each day a new beginning,
Each day part of God's plan,
Each day some special beauty,
Is waiting to be found!

We loved you when we were children,
We loved you as we grew,
We love you now each day,
God loves you even more!

Written January 19, 2012

I wrote this poem for my mom as a gift for her new apartment in her retirement home with assistance. Dad passed away. Soon after, we started looking at assisted living places for mom. It was a whirlwind, and mom was having a hard time. We all were!

"Honor your father and your mother, as the Lord your God has commanded you, so that you may live long and that it may go well with you in the land the Lord your God is giving you."
Deuteronomy 5:16

To Our Kindergarteners

The birds are singing, the flowers are here,
It's once again that time of year.
Each day we have watched you learn and grow
And now it's time to let you go.

We have worked together, played and laughed,
You even gave us presents that you wrapped.
Together we visited several places,
You all have learned to tie your laces.

The year is over, we've really had fun,
We'll remember this year long after it's done!
So, bye for now, we give you our love
And thank God for blessing us from above!

Written May 1987

My sister was a kindergarten teacher for years. She asked me to write a poem for a special program they were having for the end of the school year. My sister has a wonderful sense of humor, and she is passionate about being a good teacher. I know she had a special impact on so many children!

*"The Lord bless you
and keep you;"
Numbers 6:24*

To The Birthday Girl

A mother is a sweetheart,
A mother is a dear,
No matter how far apart,
She always holds you near!

She bathes you with her love,
She lathers you with laughter,
Each age is a miracle,
Each year is a chapter!

Take time to say thank you,
Take time to truly care,
Take time to say, "I love you!"
Your soul to really bare.

Happy birthday to my mother,
Who has lived for many years,
You have given me so much,
Love, laughter and tears!

Written on October 23, 2007

I wrote this poem for my mom's eighty-ninth birthday. My mom loved each one of us. And she loved to laugh.

"I have not stopped giving thanks for you,
remembering you in my prayers."
Ephesians 1:16

To the Bride and Groom

Angel wings and wedding bells,
Your day is a reality,
Blended hearts forevermore,
Souls as one for eternity!

Not long ago your love began
And grew through God's own grace,
Time together to know for sure,
No other could take your place!

The bride is beautiful in her gown of white
As she floats down the aisle.
The groom is handsome as he waits for her.
Their hearts unite, and they share a smile!

Loving friends and family dear
Are here with you today.
Repeat your vows and say, "I do!"
Songs of love lead the way!

God has blessed you in so many ways,
May He be with you as husband and wife,
Forever and a day together,
In union your entire life!

Written May 19, 2007

There is something so exciting and wonderful about a wedding. A long time ago I heard this saying. "Let the main thing be the main thing."

"Above all, love each other deeply,
because love covers over a multitude of sins."
1 Peter 4:8

To the Dancing Couple

Listen closely and you can hear,
The music that brought you together.
Sometime fast, sometimes slow,
The theme is repeated, "Forever!"
That Old Black Magic, Dr. Zhivago,
The waltz, the fox trot. . .and many more.
Dancing is part of your life,
Just as normal as being husband and wife!

So, as you hold each other close
And rock to the slower beat,
Remember what a special couple you are,
The ones with the dancing feet!

Written for my parents' sixtieth anniversary. They loved to dance, and they danced throughout their marriage. When I hear big band music they liked, it makes me nostalgic for their dancing.

"Let them praise his name with dancing
and make music to him with timbrel and harp."
Psalm 149:3

To the Graduate

A graduation gown, a cap upon your head,
A master's degree in your hand,
By strength and determination
To this point you were led.

Time to look back, how you've been blessed,
Depth of spirit beyond compare,
Compassion, your smile and dancing eyes
That sparkle above the rest.

God's given you wings,
You're a gift from Him,
Now it's time for you to see
What the future brings.

One thing we know,
You will be a blessing
To each and every person.
We're so proud and love you so.

A vision of heaven I can clearly see,
You at the piano playing to your heart's content.
Your dad singing with tears streaming down his face,
All the Saints around us worshiping and happy for eternity.

Written May 12, 2002

"Have I not commanded you? Be strong and courageous. Do not
be afraid; do not be discouraged, for the Lord your God will be
with you wherever you go."
Joshua 1:9

Today

I don't think you realize
How beautiful you are,
I'm talking about today,
Not a person from afar.

Your life is not a project
That one day is complete,
Unhappy until that day comes,
Often professing defeat.

God gave you His Spirit
And has a plan for you,
He wants each petal to unfold,
Now, then and later—just to name a few.

So, may you listen to His voice
That you are beautiful today,
Confidently you can go forward
And be a blessing on the way.

This is a poem we could each say to ourselves.

*"For we are God's handiwork, created in Christ Jesus to do
good works, which God prepared in advance for us to do."*
Ephesians 2:10

Together

There's a string that binds us,
It's invisible of course.
One word may move us to tears
Or to laughter just the same.
Together we are strong and growing,
Together we read God's word,
Together we learn from each other.
Our path is more beautiful than before,
Going where God leads.
Together we are strong and growing!

Written May 31, 2009

"I pray that your partnership with us in the faith may be effective in deepening your understanding of every good thing we share for the sake of Christ."
Philemon 6

Tug of War

We are in this tug of war,
Satan on one side, God on the other,
I know who wins
But it's a struggle, just the same.

You believe Satan's lies
At times unkind and cruel.
To those who surround you,
What an emptiness you are in!

People are praying
On their knees,
Pleading with God
For the outcome.

Let it be right,
Let it be true,
Oh God, let You
Be the Victory!

Written July 2, 2018

Sometimes when we are praying for someone, it feels like we are in a tug of war. I know God will win the battle one way or another!

"The Lord is not slow in keeping his promise, as some understand slowness. Instead he is patient with you, not wanting anyone to perish, but everyone to come to repentance."
2 Peter 3:9

Twinkling Lights

Jingle bells and twinkling lights,
It's that Christmas time of year.
Giving gifts and special treats
And lots of holiday cheer.

You both have seen them all,
From long ago to now.
Memories of a lifetime,
We step back and say, "Wow!"

This year is extra special,
It's a gift beyond compare.
To reflect and be thankful,
For God's daily care.

We wish you Merry Christmas,
We love you Mom and Dad.
Thank you for being you
And all these Merry Christmases we've had!

Written Christmas 2006

*"And whatever you do, whether in word or deed,
do it all in the name of the Lord Jesus,
giving thanks to God the Father through him."
Colossians 3:17*

Two Hearts

Two hearts blended as one
As though you have always been together.
Learning from each other
And discovering that it's fun.
Enthusiastic, caring and wise,
A beautiful couple with love to give.
Today you become husband and wife,
Taking with you, memories of your wedding,
Of yesterdays and all those tomorrows,
May God bless you your entire life!

Written May 19, 2007

"Out of his fullness we have all received grace
in place of grace already given."
John 1:16

Until Then

Sitting by myself, outside is dark,
I realize he really isn't here,
The silence is a stone.

I try to move and then I feel
A weight on my heart, only visible to me.
The pain, the loneliness, the ache
Sitting by myself, outside is dark.

They tell me one day will be brighter,
The sun will really shine,
And the pain almost gone—
Until then. . .

Written January 27, 2012

Written from the perspective of my mom and others who have lost
a loved one.

*"My flesh and my heart may fail,
but God is the strength of my heart
and my portion forever."
Psalm 73:26*

Use Me

I am driving on the highway of life;
Sometimes filled with joy, sometimes strife,
But always an adventure.
This prayer is a must,
Lord, use me like never before.
Don't let my life be a total bore,
Take a risk here, another one there,
The Lord will show me where.
This highway can be exciting!

I think all of us like to think we have a purpose for being here. I know I want to live life to the fullest!

"The thief comes only to steal and kill and destroy;
I have come that they may have life, and have it to the full."
John 10:10

Vessels

She held my hands
And prayed with me.
Her words washed over
My body, my soul.
It was as though
God was speaking to me!

Later I told her
How her words affected me.
She looked surprised
Said she was just a vessel.

My life is brighter
Since that day
That sweet vessel
Prayed with me.

I'm learning this more every day.
We are vessels filled with the Spirit.
Enabling us to give to others
In so many ways!

God pours out His love,
His power, His strength.
His words, His courage.
His compassion, His mercy.

It could be a ministry,
A hug, word, or tears,
We are His vessels
If we surrender to Him.

Written January 16, 2010

I was in a 6:30 AM Bible study at my church. In our first meeting of the year, we had a morning of prayer. We met in the chapel. It was quiet, calm, and peaceful with soft piano music playing. It really was a time for quiet prayer, and it was wonderful. There were two gals who are gifted in prayer who were there for anyone who wanted to pray. In my mind I said, "I'll let the others go." Then I found myself walking up to one of them, and this is what I said, "I can't quit writing." She didn't laugh. We prayed about that and about someone I am praying for who is on the brink of believing. Having her words wash over me and being anointed with oil were new experiences for me, and they were beautiful moments I carry with me every day.

"But we have this treasure in jars of clay to show that this all-surpassing power is from God and not from us."
2 Corinthians 4:7

We Are Women!

God has a plan,
God has a way,
To reveal to us,
Who we are today.

He gently reminds
Today is a gift.
To pray and to do,
To give our soul a lift!

We are women, we are real,
We are proud of who we are,
God, give us the strength
To not wonder far!

We women form a circle
To learn and to pray,
May we help each other
Find God's will every day!

Written October 25, 2007

"'Many women do noble things, but you surpass them all.'
Charm is deceptive, and beauty is fleeting; but a woman
who fears the Lord is to be praised."
Proverbs 31: 29-30

We Knew This Day Would Come

We knew this day would come
And yet, our hearts cry out for time to stand still,
To the little boy with boots and toys, we now say our good-bye.
We know it's right, but why must it be so hard?

A little boy—then a teen—tall and lots of fun.
We'll never forget that eighth grade race,
You really shocked us when you won,
"It must be a gift from God!"

Then time to drive—don't be afraid,
We tell ourselves over and over,
Friends were here, and games were played
And laughter filled the air!

No more searching for your form
On the grassy cross-country fields.
Instead, studying at college and living in a dorm
And having the time of your life!

We will miss these moments—race after race,
Memories stored in the future to ponder.
More than that, we will miss your smiling face,
The tender heart and the laughter,
From little boy to grown up man,
We love you our son!

Written for our son on his graduation from high school. I was very
nostalgic about our first child leaving home.

"But seek first his kingdom and his righteousness, and all these
things will be given to you as well."
Matthew 6:33

Welcome to The World

Welcome to the world,
It is a beautiful day.
Now that you are here,
We already love you in so many ways!

You are part of a wonderful family,
Fun as they can be,
They will play and laugh with you,
It will be great, you will see!

God made you very special.
You've been given your name,
No one else on this earth,
Is like you or exactly the same!

Welcome to the world!

Written July 22, 2009

"For you created my inmost being; you knit me together in my mother's womb. I praise you because I am fearfully and wonderfully made; your works are wonderful, I know that full well. My frame was not hidden from you when I was made in the secret place, when I was woven together in the depth of the earth. Your eyes saw my unformed body; all the days ordained for me were written in your book before one of them came to be."
Psalm 139:13-16

What I Appreciate About You

You are my cuddle in the morning,
My kiss at night before I close my eyes.
You are the strength beside me,
Never stronger than when we are on our knees!
You were the voice saying, "I do!"
Until death do us part!
One hand, one heart!
You were the hand that held mine,
When a child that was ours
Was taken back to heaven.
You were the voice that said,
"You're pregnant! God has heard our prayers!"
The husband beside me,
When our son came in the world!
The one I looked into your eyes
And said, "I love you!" when
Our next child was ready to be born!
You were smiling next to me,
When our youngest was placed in my arms,
You're so strong, yet not afraid
To shed a tear or give a hug.
God gave you the voice of an angel!
And nothing could be sweeter
Than spending eternity with you!

Written to my husband on April 28, 2002

"Do everything in love."
1 Corinthians 16:14

With Thanksgiving

I look back on the day you were born,
I was so excited—our third, a baby girl.
Enthusiasm, sparkle, energy galore,
Having you around always kept our lives in a whirl.

When you were small, I smiled at you and said,
"Let's take a nap—it's getting late!"
So, you would put your little hand in mine,
Those times were great.

I pray the bond between us
Will still be there when I'm old.
With thanksgiving and amazement
I will watch your life unfold!

Written August 5, 1994

*"But as for you, continue in what you have learned and have
become convinced of, because you know those from whom you
learned it, and how from infancy you have known the Holy
Scriptures, which are able to make you wise for salvation through
faith in Christ Jesus."*
2 Timothy 3:14-15

Wood Guy Tom and Shop Gal Kathie

You're an adorable pair,
Old-fashioned you say,
Dates every Thursday night,
With a coupon—you're on your way!

Tom—reverently "opening" the wood,
Creating with your heart
Furniture, toys, games and more.
They are wonderful from the start!

Kathie—with a smile on your face,
Sharing Tom's passion for wood,
Heavenly creations they are.
Tom's full-time hobby if he could!

Wood Guy Tom and Shop Gal Kathie,
May you continue to create
Giving praise to our Father,
Loving those Thursday night dates!

Written January 24, 2010

I met Tom and Kathie when I was looking for someone to write/ etch/carve my grandson's name on the little rocking chair we gave him for Christmas. I searched and searched, and found Tom. I knew it was a God-thing when I went to their home, and Tom's wife walked into the wood shop and said, "Hi, I'm shop gal Kathie." Yes, we even spell our names alike. They are a cute Christian couple, and we could have talked for hours. What a neat way to discover Christian friends.

"You are my friends if you do what I command."
John 15:14

Written on Our Hearts

I don't know how, I don't know when,
But it is written on our hearts.
To be messengers of God,
To give His love unselfishly,
To pray for others endlessly,
To be His hands and feet.

God alone knows you
As no one else possibly can,
He loves you and wants to hold your hand.
To walk with you—however long the journey,
However deep the path.

He will wrap His arms around you
And wipe away your tears.
He is the beginning and the end,
He lives in us, my friend!

Written December 17, 2009

*"This is the covenant I will establish with the people of Israel
after that time, declares the Lord.
I will put my laws in their minds
and write them on their hearts.
I will be their God,
and they will be my people."
Hebrews 8:10*

You Are Going to Be a Mom

You are having a baby,
Baby cribs and baby toys
Are dancing in your head.
The countdown is on,
A new life you'll be holding.
As incredible as it sounds,
You are going to be a mom!

Written November 2, 2008

"Children are a heritage from the Lord,
offspring a reward from him."
Psalm 127:3

You

You are wonderful,
You are smart,
You have energy,
You have heart!

You listen to God each day,
You reach out to others and pray,
You know just what to say,
You rely on Jesus as The Way!

You use your gifts so wisely,
You know God has a plan,
You have a golden soul,
You help others if you can!

You are wonderful,
You are smart,
You have energy,
You have heart!

Written March 22, 2007 I say, "Way to go!" if you are living your life this way!

"Look to the Lord and his strength; seek his face always."
1 Chronicles 16:11

You Wear It Well

With a pretty face
And a spirit that's bright,
You live each day
And make it fun!

You love to talk,
There are stories to tell.
Going afternoon dancing,
Taking food to the sick.

Ninety years! You wear it well!
What makes you special?
Giving, sharing, caring,
You live your faith!

October 23, 2008

Written for my mom for her ninetieth birthday. Did I mention she is ninety years young? She and my dad still lived at home. They loved to cook, dance, and have fun! Now, that is inspiring!

"Because your love is better than life, my lips will glorify you."
Psalm 63:3

You Were There

You were there
When our first was just a dream,
And then one by one
God placed them in our arms.
We laughed, we cried, and realized the truth.
It is our three who captivate us by their charms!

To be a father is a gift from God above,
A challenge beyond compare.
Integrity, faith, and love,
Are attributes we share.

Now three more special people
Walk the path that we have trod.
Not to our credit alone,
But by the grace of God!

Written to my husband for Father's Day 2003. Our children were grown, and it was easy to look back and appreciate that they were gifts from God and that I so appreciated getting to share that experience with him.

*"But to each one of us grace has been given as
Christ apportioned it."*
Ephesians 4:7

You're Falling in Love With Your Flock

We can hear it in your voice,
We can see it in your eyes,
God is giving you this love
And He is making you wise.

Today you couldn't hide it,
The love for each soul.
So, to our shepherd,
The flock loves you back!

Written October 1, 1989

I wrote this poem about a minister who was new in his position.

"Keep watch over yourselves and all the flock of which the Holy
Spirit has made you overseers. Be shepherds of the church of God,
which he bought with his own blood."
Acts 20:28

You're Special

To our firstborn, so strong and still a boy.
Always ready to smile and talk,
To us you are a joy!
You're our child, you're special!

To our second, caring and quiet,
So many things to create.
We can't wait to see them all!
You're our child, you're special!

To our youngest, energetic and bright,
With Jesus's dancing eyes,
We know you are His light!
You're our child, you're special!

I wrote this poem to express to our children that we love each one of them, and we appreciate that each one is unique.

"And whatever you do, whether in word or deed, do it all in the name of the Lord Jesus, giving thanks to God the Father through him."
Colossians 3:17

Your Child

"A baby is God's opinion the world should go on"
He soon is going to give you a daughter or a son,
Baby smiles to brighten your days,
Enriched lives in so many ways!
A mother and a father in a few months you will be,
The most beautiful child in the world—You will see!

I received a plaque a long time ago that said, "A baby is God's opinion the world should go on." That is such a wonderful message! Later, I discovered these words are a quote from Carl Sandberg. Over the years I have shared this poem with several people, and it has been so much fun sharing it with them.

"Children's children are a crown to the aged,
and parents are the pride of their children."
Proverbs 17:6

Your Future

As you face the future
Putting one foot in front of the other,
Living your life for Him.
May you be blessed richly:
With love,
With peace,
With laughter,
With joy,
And know that I am one of many
Praying for you daily,
Loving you for who you are.
Cherishing the moment,
Looking to the future,
Living our lives for Him!

Written April 2, 2012

"But you are a chosen people, a royal priesthood, a holy nation,
God's special possession, that you may declare the praises of him
who called you out of darkness into his wonderful light."
1 Peter 2:9

Your Soul Is Weary

I know your soul is weary with sorrow.
You ask for strength to make it through hard days,
Although many surrounding you with caring hearts;
They try, but can't take your pain away.

Of this I am certain—One day it happens,
You reach for the Savior's sweet embrace
And the angels are praising with heavenly songs.
You and your loved one are face to face!

Tears of joy spring from your eyes,
The lift of your spirit has no end.
Together again, this time for keeps,
With thankful hearts, praises you send!

Written January 28, 2012

Several people close to me have lost a loved one not too long ago, and they have moments of painfully missing that person. I know God understands. I pray that we all can picture the first people to greet us in heaven will be our loved ones who are already there. In the meantime, God holds our hand.

"My soul is weary with sorrow;
strengthen me according to your word."
Psalm 119:28

GOING FORWARD ON YOUR JOURNEY

I pray that as you live each day, there are words from scripture or maybe even words from one of these poems that will touch your heart and brighten your day.

These words from scripture beautifully express what I wish for each one of you.

May God bless your journey!

"Let the name of the Lord be praised,
both now and forevermore."
Psalm 113:2

CPSIA information can be obtained
at www.ICGtesting.com
Printed in the USA
FFHW011023100419
51644984-57066FF